Beautiful Food

Photograph: Thom DeSanto

Half title page: *Peach Parfait Cake, p. 126*; this page: *Salade Chinoise, p. 35*.

Carved Fruits, p. 67.

Photograph: Larry Couzens

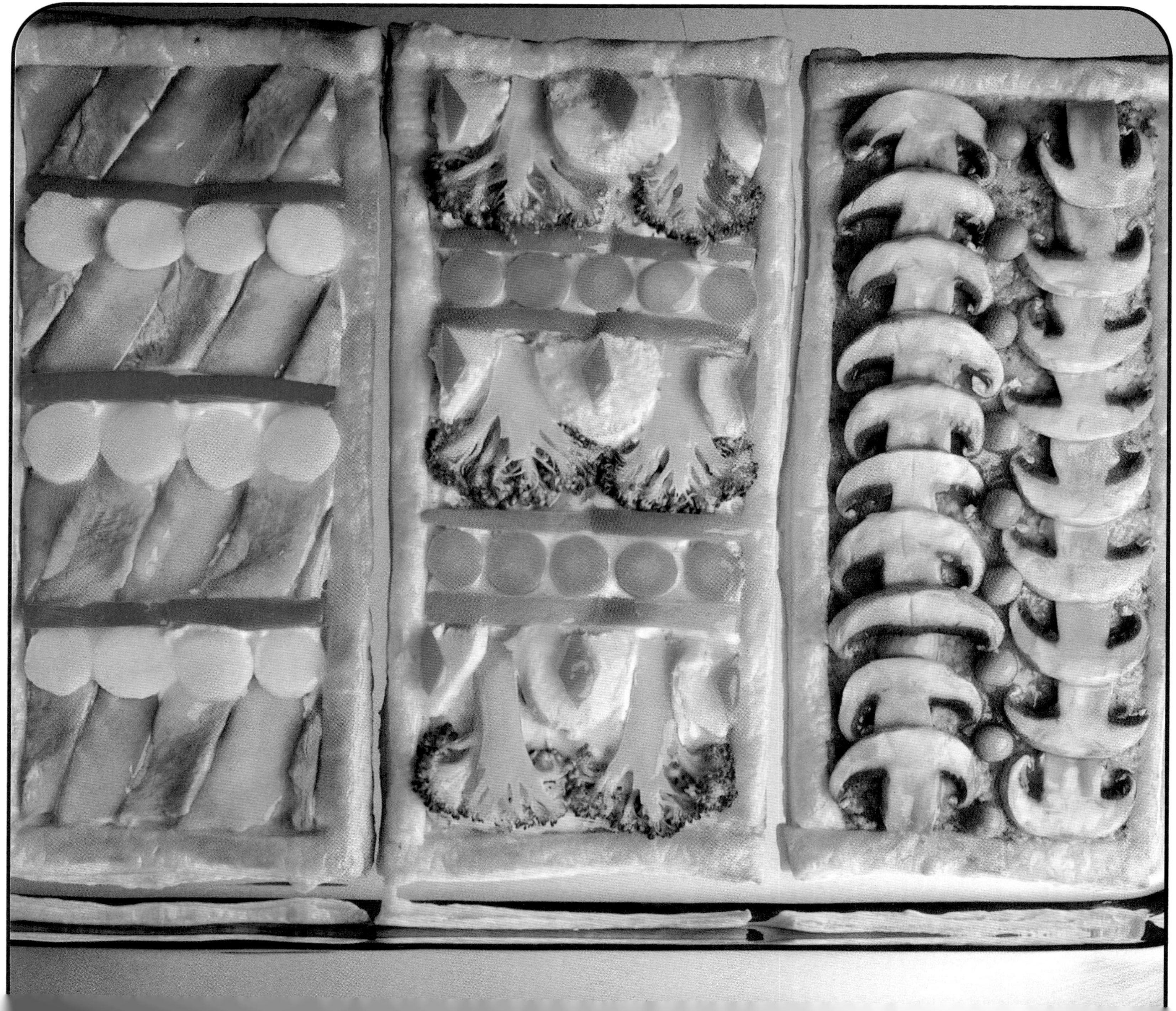

Savory Vegetable Tarts, p. 22.

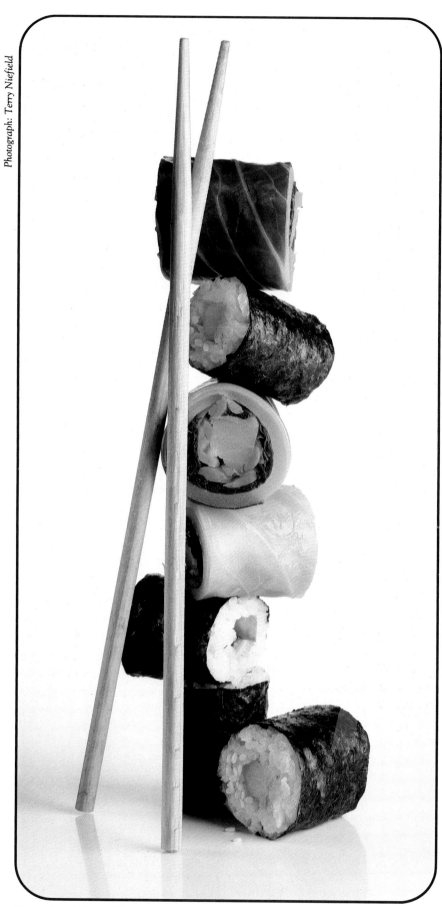

Vegetarian Sushi, p. 72.

Glazed Lobster with Saffron-Lobster Salad, p. 113.

Salad-Filled Pies, p. 103.

Beautiful Food

A Cookbook by Jim Fobel

A Genie Book

 VAN NOSTRAND REINHOLD COMPANY
NEW YORK CINCINNATI TORONTO LONDON MELBOURNE

Book designed by Allan Mogel

Book illustrated by Jim Fobel

All food styling for photography by Jim Fobel with the exception of "Lovely Layered Cheeses" (styled by Lucy Wing) and "Salad-Filled Pie" (styled by Richmond Ellis)

Stencil designs for "Sugar-Sifted Holiday Cookies and Brownies" by J. K. Boleach

Cover design by Allan Mogel

Cover photograph by Terry Niefield; back cover photograph by John Garetti

Special thanks to Richmond Ellis for his assistance

The recipes appearing on pages 22, 27, 35, 53, 67, 103, 126 are reprinted with permission from the October 1980, November 1981, January 1981, April 1981, August 1982, July 1982, and July 1981 issues of *Food & Wine* magazine, © 1980, 1981, 1982 by The International Review of Food & Wine Associates. The recipes on pages 18, 49, 59, 80, 83, 135, 151, 157, 159, 168 have appeared in slightly different form in *Decorating & Crafts Ideas* magazine.

Published by Van Nostrand Reinhold Company Inc.
135 West 50th Street
New York, New York 10020

Fleet Publishers
1410 Birchmount Road
Scarborough, Ontario M1P 2E7, Canada

Van Nostrand Reinhold
480 Latrobe Street
Melbourne, Victoria 3000, Australia

Van Nostrand Reinhold Company Limited
Molly Millars Lane
Wokingham, Berkshire RG11 2PY, England

16 15 14 13 12 11 10 9 8 7 6 5 4 3 2 1

Library of Congress Cataloging in Publication Data

Fobel, Jim.
    Beautiful food.

    Includes index.
    1. Cookery. 2. Menus. 3. Entertaining. I. Title.
TX652.F58   1983   641.5   83-3492
ISBN 0-442-22730-2

For Mary, who taught me to cook with sherry

Contents

Introduction

I can't compromise. The more cookbooks I see devoted to the preparation of "meals in minutes," the more I find myself savoring every moment I put into creating beautiful food.

Perhaps my background has something to do with it. In college, I majored in fine arts—painting and ceramics. When I first moved to New York City ten years ago, I arrived with every intention of pursuing my career as an artist. No one could have convinced me then that, ultimately, I would switch my main interest from paint and clay to meat and potatoes. I was secure as a painter and cooking was merely my pastime, a way to relax and escape.

Once food became my main interest, though, it quickly became evident that I had not abandoned my love for creating objects that please the eye as well as the palate. Without my being aware of it at the time, the five years that I had studied ceramics had formed a unique foundation for my work with foods. I was able to apply the principles of art and science that I had learned while making pottery to the making of tasty dishes to be eaten at the table.

Back in the early 1960s, I performed a series of experiments calculated to formulate clays and ceramic glazes that naturally complemented each other. Each time that I began to experiment with a new formula, I kept exact records. Weights, measurements, temperatures, equipment, and procedures were all carefully noted, for once I had perfected the formula, others had to be able to duplicate it time and time again from my records.

My first experimenting began the day I uncovered a pocket of highly unusual gray earth in California's San Fernando Valley. I hauled as much of it as I could back to the ceramics lab. There I worked it into a glaze, applied it to clay, put it through the fire, and was ecstatic with the result—the finished pot had a beautiful stonelike surface flecked throughout with gray and white. I then began adding various minerals and natural chemicals to the basic glaze, each time changing its color, surface texture, density, melting point, and ability to adhere to the clay beneath. At the same time, I began to work on developing a chocolate brown clay that I felt would show off the glaze to its best.

Once the clay and glaze formulas had been perfected and committed to paper, they worked with exactly the same results no matter who tested them. It was through such creative experimentation that I was able to achieve such happy results, but it was through the scientific process that they could be reproduced over and over again. The Chocolate Brown Clay Body and the San Fernando Gray Glaze that I developed are now formulas, or recipes if you will, that anyone can duplicate; a marriage of art and science there for all to enjoy. So it is with the recipes in this book.

What do painting and pottery have to do with food? Plenty. Your kitchen is your lab; the stove and refrigerator are your kilns, a chunk of pastry or a stack of platters are your canvases, and raw ingredients are your paint or clay. In food preparation, a metamorphosis takes place that transforms raw ingredients into finished edible creations, sometimes through heat transmission, sometimes by means of refrigeration, sometimes through motion. The more that you know about the science of food, the more accurately you will be able to predict what will happen to the food when you experiment.

If you want to learn more about food through recipe development, make a series of tests like I did with my glaze experiments. Pretend that a bag of flour is the basis of your experiment, your "mother earth." Most of you probably already know that bread is made from flour and water, but how many know that when salt and fat are added, pastry is formed? Add sugar and eggs, and cake is produced. If your liquid is heated before the flour and eggs are added, cream puffs are created. Add puréed potatoes to the cream-puff paste and you have *gnocchi,* or add puréed seafood to make *quenelles.* The possibilities in this culinary chain are endless.

You might try experimenting with the basic biscuit formula, which includes flour, fat, baking powder, salt, and liquid. To begin, you might decide to use broth for the liquid. To complement that flavor, you could try using a combination of rye and white flours and add a spoonful of ground seeds or crumbled herbs for flavor. For the fat, you might try rendered duck fat for the usual butter, shortening, or lard. Bacon fat, goose fat, or olive oil might work as well. Each ingredient that you use will react differently with the other recipe components.

After the biscuits have been baked, you might find that although they have a delicious, addicting flavor, they haven't risen enough: the combination of flours that you used might have been wrong, you may not have added enough baking powder, or perhaps, you added too much liquid. On the other hand, you may have invented a new rye-flavored crust without even knowing it. Analyze its qualities. Decide whether its best characteristics are worth pursuing. As you do so, keep in mind that the correct application of heat or refrigeration is very important because it, too, will contribute to the finished product.

Finally, when you have invented the biscuit that you are happy with and have kept exact records, you will have a formula that others can follow to achieve the same results that you did. Be aware, however, that the flour, just like the earth, will vary from region to region.

Experimentation takes time. I have been working on some of the recipes in this book for almost ten years and they will continue to evolve for many more.

The creative possibilities with the projects in *Beautiful Food* are infinite. You can cut fruits and vegetables into a variety of shapes and combine them with a multitude of other ingredients. Or, use your digital dexterity to model bread dough into an edible work of art. You might want to use the Savory Vegetable Tarts as the inspiration for a dessert made with fresh fruit over a lemon mousse. If you want to make your own version of the Lovely Layered Cheeses, keep in mind that there are many other types of cheeses available that could be used instead of my suggestions, and, of course, you can flavor the layers as you please. You can make a personal antipasto jar, using your own design ideas, by following the directions included here.

Beautiful food has always had an important place in our lives. For generations, birthdays and anniversaries have been celebrated with the classic, decorated layer cake. And, from the moment that chocolate making was perfected, people have been molding it into decorative shapes. Give a chef a piece of pastry, and he will make a pie with a fluted edge. I myself cannot resist the temptation to stamp Aztec designs of chili paste onto corn tortillas for a party and neither can I stop myself from sprinkling paprika in lines across a loaf of garlic bread or chopped parsley over pasta.

Today, elaborate food seems to be restricted to expensive caterers, hotels, restaurants, and first-class ocean liners. But, it need not remain that way. You can prepare a showstopping, edible centerpiece from the formulas included here to cater your own party. The rewards of such personal achievement are tremendous.

Since the way that people taste food is affected by the way that it looks, I predict that your guests will rave about the creations that you prepare from this book. Whether you want to celebrate a special occasion during the summer, fall, winter, or spring, *Beautiful Food* is intended to be a springboard for your own creativity.

Jim Fobel
New York City, 1983

1
Appetizers

Mosaic Shrimp-and-Salmon Mousse

(Photograph on page 90)

Once in a while it's fun to splurge and entertain in an elegant fashion. When that mood strikes, you can be sure that this shrimp-and-salmon mousse, crowned with a mosaic design of fresh vegetables, will be a show stopper. And, it can be prepared the day before you want to serve it, leaving you free the day of the big event to prepare other foods and organize details.

During the morning of the day before your party, prepare the vegetables for the mosaic pattern and line the bowl with them. Then cover the bowl and keep it in the refrigerator until you prepare the mousse. Once the mousse is mixed and poured into the lined bowl, all you need to do is cover it and refrigerate overnight.

For a party for more than ten or twelve people, I find serving food buffet-style the most convenient, and this savory mousse, served as a first course, is a festive way to begin the celebration, particularly if you are entertaining outdoors. To balance the menu and expand the buffet, you might want to add any of or all the following foods: Mushroom-Filled Salad Pie (see recipe, p. 103), onion tarts, crudités, lobster-stuffed tomatoes, a smoked turkey, an apricot-stuffed loin of pork, a platter of cold sliced meats, parslied new potatoes, sesame bread sticks with sweet butter, a fruit salad or arrangement of seasonal fruit, and a cheese assortment. As a beverage, champagne or a fruit punch (see recipes, p. 142) would be an ideal complement.

Mosaic Shrimp-and-Salmon Mousse
SERVES 32 TO 40 AS A FIRST COURSE

Vegetables:
- 4 medium-size to large carrots, peeled
- 2 medium-size yellow summer squash or 12 yellow wax beans
- 1 tablespoon salt
- 1½ pounds medium-size green beans, ends trimmed and beans cut into 3-inch lengths
- 2 large red bell peppers, quartered, cored, and deribbed
- 32 large pitted black olives, sliced
- ½ cup shelled or frozen peas
- 2 large green bell peppers, halved, cored, deribbed, and cut into ¼-inch-wide strips 2 to 3 inches long
- 2 medium-size white turnips, peeled and cut into ½-inch-wide strips 1 inch long
- 1 tablespoon vegetable oil

Shrimp-and-Salmon Mousse:
- 4 bottles (8 ounces each) clam juice or fish stock
- 1½ cups finely chopped onion (1 large)
- 2 pounds small to medium-size shrimp, shelled and deveined
- 3 pounds fresh salmon steaks, cut 1 inch thick, skinned, boned, and cut into 1-inch cubes
- ⅓ cup fresh lemon juice
- ½ cup dry white wine
- 7 envelopes (¼ ounce each) unflavored gelatin
- 1 pint sour cream
- ¾ cup mayonnaise, preferably homemade (see recipe, p. 25)
- 1 can (6 ounces) tomato paste
- ⅓ cup well-drained prepared horseradish
- ¾ cup (lightly packed) finely minced fresh dill
- 2 teaspoons salt (optional)
- 1 teaspoon freshly ground pepper

Garnish (optional):
- 2 large lemons
- 14 medium-size to large cooked, shelled, deveined shrimp sprigs of fresh dill

1. Cut the vegetables: Cut one round of carrot that is ¼ inch thick; reserve. Cut the remaining carrots into sticks that measure 3 inches long, ½ inch wide, and ¼ inch thick. Trim the ends from the yellow squash and cut them in half lengthwise; scoop out the center portions, leaving ¼-inch-thick shells; discard the center portions. Cut the squash into strips that measure 3 inches long, ½ inch wide, and ¼ inch thick. If using yellow wax beans, simply trim them into 3-inch lengths.

2. Prepare the vegetables: In a large, heavy pot, combine about 2 quarts of water and the 1 tablespoon salt and bring to a boil. Cook each vegetable separately, following the chart below. Remove the vegetables with a slotted spoon as they are done, transfer them to a colander, and rinse them under cold running water to stop them from cooking further. (Since vegetables, depending on their age, may require more or less cooking time, occasionally taste one for doneness as they cook.)

Carrots	5-8 minutes
Yellow squash	1 minute
Green beans	5-8 minutes
Red or green bell peppers	3-5 minutes
Peas	4-5 minutes
White turnips	6-8 minutes

3. Line the bowl with the vegetable-mosaic design: Choose a 4-quart, noncorrosive bowl that measures approximately 9 inches in diameter and is about 6 inches deep. Using the oil, generously coat the entire inner surface of the bowl. Keeping the vegetables in separate piles, begin to create the design

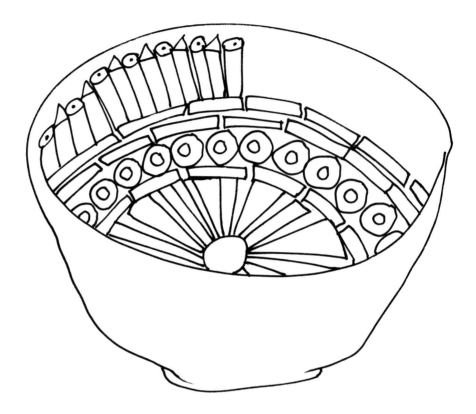

(refer to the photo and the illustration as guides). Place the reserved carrot round in the center of the bottom of the bowl. Pressing each vegetable firmly against the bowl as you position it, lay a strip of yellow squash or a wax bean, with a strip of green pepper on each side, along the bottom of the bowl so that they radiate like arms from the carrot round. Cut a triangular shape from a piece of red pepper to fit next to it and then repeat the procedure all around the inside bottom of the bowl. Next, add a horizontal ring of green pepper strips around the upper edge of the design. Arrange a ring of olive slices above the green pepper ring and insert a green pea into the center of each. Add another horizontal ring of green pepper and top with a ring of turnip strips. Finally, alternate, vertically, strips of carrot and the 3-inch lengths of green bean. Being careful not to disturb the designs, cover and set the bowl aside while you make the mousse.

4. Prepare the mousse: In a large, heavy, noncorrosive pot or Dutch oven, combine the clam juice or fish stock with the onion and place it over moderately high heat. Bring the mixture to a boil, reduce the heat slightly, and simmer for 5 minutes. Add the shrimp and salmon; increase the heat to high and, stirring frequently, bring to a boil. Reduce the heat to low and simmer, stirring occasionally, for 2 to 3 minutes, or until the shrimp and salmon are cooked.

5. Place a large colander over a large bowl, and, working in batches if necessary, drain the seafood in the colander, catching the juices in the bowl. Shake the colander up and down several times to extract as much liquid as possible. Spread the seafood over a large platter so that it cools quickly. Measure the liquid. You should have 4 cups. If you have more, discard some; if you have less, add enough water to make 4 cups. Place the liquid along with the lemon juice in the large pot or Dutch oven in which you cooked the seafood.

6. Pour the wine into a medium-size bowl and add the gelatin; stir briefly. Add 1 cup of the liquid from the pot. Add the gelatin mixture to the pot and bring it just to a simmer over moderate heat, stirring occasionally. Allow the liquid to rest for 5 minutes to let any fat from the salmon rise to the top. Blot the fat up with a paper towel. Then place the liquid in a bowl and either set it in the refrigerator or place it in a larger bowl filled with ice and stir frequently until the liquid has the consistency of syrup. If the liquid should happen to gel completely, heat it briefly and then rechill it to the syrupy stage.

7. Meanwhile, **purée the seafood:** Carefully pick over the salmon, discarding any bones present. Then, working in batches, purée the salmon and shrimp in a food processor or blender (you should have about 8 cups). In a large bowl, combine the sour cream, mayonnaise, tomato paste, horseradish, and dill. Stir to blend well. Blend in the seafood purée and add the optional salt and the pepper. Fold in the syrupy gelatin mixture until well blended. Uncover the vegetable-lined bowl and carefully ladle the mixture into it, taking care not to disturb the design. Cover and chill overnight.

8. To serve: Remove the mousse from the refrigerator and, if necessary, cut away and discard any vegetables extending above the mousse. Moisten a serving platter with a little cold water so that the mousse can be centered after unmolding it. Then dip the bowl into a larger bowl or sinkful of hot water for 20 to 30 seconds and invert it onto the platter, tapping it sharply if necessary. If it does not unmold, dip the bowl back into the hot water and try again. If any of the vegetables have stuck to the bowl, replace them on the mousse.

9. Using a knife or a zester, remove evenly spaced, lengthwise strips of peel from the lemons and discard. Then cut the lemons crosswise into slices about ¼ inch thick. Arrange them in a border around the mousse and top each with a cooked whole shrimp and a sprig of dill.

Savory Vegetable Tarts

(Photograph on page 4)

If you have a colorful spectrum of ingredients on hand, all sorts of exciting, kaleidoscopic designs can be made to top the following tart shells for a dazzling display of artistry.

Each tart begins with a crisp butter-pastry shell that is spread with pâté or a flavored mayonnaise. Cross-sections of vegetables and mushrooms interspersed with thin strips of chicken and duck are then arranged on top in geometric patterns. For a gleaming "finish," a glaze is brushed over the whole. Inventing the designs can be half the fun of making these tarts, but you can also simply follow the photograph of this project.

Although the following butter-pastry recipe makes four tart shells, the ingredients in the individual tart recipes have been calculated to make only two tarts, so that you can try your hand at making two different kinds of tarts rather than four of a kind. If you'd rather make all four the same, simply double the amount of ingredients called for. It is important that the glaze used to finish the tarts be freshly made and still hot, so assemble all the tarts first and then glaze them all at once.

To cut the tarts at serving time, use a long, heavy, sharp knife and apply pressure to it along the back of the blade (rather than using a sawing motion) so as not to disturb the designs.

Mushroom Tarts
MAKES TWO 5- BY 10-INCH TARTS

14 *large mushrooms of equal size (1½ to 2 inches in diameter)*
2 *tablespoons fresh lemon juice*
2 *baked Butter-Pastry Tart Shells (recipe follows)*

2 *cups Mushroom Pâté (recipe follows)*
18 *cooked green peas (instructions follow)*
4 *tablespoons hot Glaze (recipe follows)*

1. Trim off ⅛ inch from the stem end of each mushroom and discard. Leaving the stems attached, trim away two sides of each mushroom cap, leaving only the center portions (reserve the trimmings for the Mushroom Pâté). Cut each center portion into three vertical slices.

2. Place 2 cups of water and the lemon juice in a medium-size, noncorrosive saucepan and bring to a boil. Add the mushrooms; when the water resumes boiling, cover the pan and simmer them for about 3 minutes, or until tender. Drain thoroughly and reserve.

3. Using a knife or spatula, gently spread each tart shell with about 1 cup of the Mushroom Pâté, bringing it out just to the edge. Referring to the photograph, make two rows of overlapping mushroom slices on each tart, the second row facing in the opposite direction from the first, and separate the rows with a line of nine peas.

4. Evenly spoon half the Glaze over each tart. Cool the tarts to room temperature and then chill them, uncovered, for at least an hour. If necessary to hold them longer, cover loosely with aluminum foil.

Broccoli and Chicken Tarts
MAKES TWO 5- BY 10-INCH TARTS

2 baked Butter-Pastry Tart Shells (recipe follows)

½ cup Lemon Mayonnaise (recipe follows)

6 cooked broccoli flowerets, each 2 inches long (instructions follow)

1 can (4 ounces) pimientos, rinsed and drained

1 whole, cooked, skinless, boneless chicken breast, halved lengthwise (8 ounces)

16 strips cooked green pepper, each ¼ inch wide by 2¼ inches long (instructions follow)

20 small, cooked carrot slices, ¼ inch thick (instructions follow)

4 tablespoons hot Glaze (recipe follows)

1. Using a spoon, gently spread each tart shell with ¼ cup of the Lemon Mayonnaise, bringing it out just to the edge.

2. Cut through the broccoli flowerets, including the stem sections, to create twelve cross-sections. If necessary, trim away a small amount of green from the underside of each so that they will lie flat. Cut the pimiento into twelve diamond shapes, each about ¾ inch in length. Cut each chicken breast half across the grain into slices ¼ inch thick. Trim six of the most attractive slices into half-ovals that will fit neatly between the broccoli slices. Finally, trim six more of the chicken slices into half-ovals and then cut them in half lengthwise. (Reserve any remaining chicken for another use.)

3. Referring to the photograph, arrange half the prepared chicken and vegetables on each tart shell and evenly spoon with half the Glaze. Cool the tarts to room temperature and then chill them, uncovered, for at least 1 hour; if necessary to hold them longer, cover loosely with aluminum foil.

Snow-Pea and Duck Tarts
MAKES TWO 5- BY 10-INCH TARTS

2 baked Butter-Pastry Tart Shells (recipe follows)

½ cup Oriental Sesame Mayonnaise (recipe follows)

1 whole, cooked, skinless, boneless duck breast (from a 5-pound duck), halved lengthwise (see Note)

8 small, fresh or canned, peeled water chestnuts

20 cooked snow peas (instructions follow)

12 strips cooked red bell pepper or pimiento, each ¼ inch wide by 2¼ inches long (instructions follow)

4 tablespoons hot Glaze (recipe follows)

Note: If you don't feel like roasting a duck, you can usually buy one already cooked from a Chinese restaurant or grocery store.

1. Using a spoon, gently spread each tart shell with ¼ cup of the sesame mayonnaise, bringing it out just to the edge.

2. Cut the duck breast on the bias into ⅛-inch-thick slices that are about 2 inches long. Slice each water chestnut crosswise into three rounds.

3. Referring to the photograph, alternate the duck strips with the snow peas, layering them diagonally across each tart and trimming them as necessary to fit neatly on the tart. Add the water chestnuts and pepper strips as shown.

4. Evenly spoon half the Glaze over each tart. Cool them to room temperature and then chill them, uncovered, for at least an hour. If necessary to hold them longer, cover loosely with aluminum foil.

Butter-Pastry Tart Shells
MAKES FOUR 5- BY 10-INCH SHELLS

3 cups all-purpose flour
½ teaspoon salt
1 cup (2 sticks) unsalted butter, chilled and thinly sliced

⅓ cup vegetable shortening
about ½ cup ice water
1 egg yolk for glazing

1. Make the pastry: In a large mixing bowl, combine the flour and salt. Using a pastry blender or two knives, quickly cut in the butter and shortening until the mixture resembles coarse meal. (If the butter is warm, the pastry will not be flaky; chill if necessary.)

2. Sprinkle ¼ cup of the ice water over the flour mixture and stir rapidly with a fork. Continuing to mix rapidly, sprinkle enough of the remaining water over the pastry so that it can be gathered in a ball. (Use additional drops of ice water if necessary, but do not overwork or the pastry shells will be tough when baked.) Divide the dough in half. Flatten each half and wrap tightly; refrigerate for at least 2 hours or as long as overnight.

3. Make the tart shells: Preheat the oven to 400°F. From paper, cut a 5- by 10-inch rectangle to use as a pattern. Working on a lightly floured surface, quickly roll out half the pastry (leave the remainder in the refrigerator) to a 12-inch square that is about ⅛ inch thick or slightly more. Using a paring knife to cut around the pattern, cut two rectangles of dough. Also cut out eight ¼-inch-wide strips—four that are 9½ inches long and four that are 5 inches long. (Refrigerate the pastry scraps for another use.) Using a lightly floured spatula, transfer the two rectangles to an ungreased baking sheet.

4. Beat the egg yolk with 1 teaspoon water in a cup to make a glaze. Using a small brush or your fingertip, moisten the top outer edge of one pastry rectangle. Then, edge the rectangle with four corresponding strips of pastry, laying the strips flat so that a ⅛-inch-deep rim is formed around the rectangle. Brush the top of the rim with more of the glaze. Repeat to make a second tart shell. Cover and refrigerate while you make the second two tart shells.

5. Remove the first two shells from the refrigerator and prick the bottoms of all four shells all over with a fork. Bake them for 12 to 15 minutes, or until golden brown and crisp, pricking them again if necessary to prevent the bottom from bubbling up. Let the shells cool for 5 minutes, carefully transfer them to a wire rack, and allow to cool thoroughly. If loosely covered with aluminum foil, the shells may be left at room temperature for one day.

Mushroom Pâté
MAKES ABOUT 2 CUPS (enough for two tarts)

¼ cup unsalted butter
3 tablespoons minced shallots or onion
3 cups coarsely chopped mushrooms (see Note)
½ cup dry vermouth or white wine

1 egg yolk
1 cup chopped, cooked, dark chicken meat
1 teaspoon fresh lemon juice
½ teaspoon salt
¼ teaspoon freshly ground pepper

Note: You can use the mushroom trimmings from the Mushroom Tart, broken mushrooms, or a combination of both.

1. Melt the butter in a large, heavy, noncorrosive skillet set over moderate heat; add the shallots and sauté until translucent, about 5 minutes. Stir in the mushrooms and cook, stirring occasionally, until they have released their juices, 3 to 5 minutes. Continue cooking, without stirring, until the liquid has evaporated. Add the vermouth or white wine and cook until the liquid has reduced to about 1 tablespoon.

2. Combine the hot mushroom mixture with the egg yolk, chicken, lemon juice, salt, and pepper in the container of a food processor or blender and coarsely purée. Cover and refrigerate for at least 1 hour.

Basic Mayonnaise
All the ingredients for this recipe should be at room temperature before beginning, or the emulsion will not take.
MAKES ABOUT 1 CUP (enough for four tarts)

2 egg yolks, at room temperature
1 tablespoon fresh lemon juice or cider vinegar
1 teaspoon salt

freshly ground pepper to taste
½ cup olive oil
½ cup vegetable oil

1. Fill a deep, medium-size mixing bowl with hot water and let it rest for 2 or 3 minutes. Pour out the water and thoroughly dry the bowl. Add the egg yolks, lemon juice or vinegar, salt, and pepper; beat with a whisk or an electric mixer until blended.

2. Combine the two oils and, beating constantly with a whisk or an electric mixer at medium speed, begin to add the mixture a drop at a time to the egg yolks, making sure that each drop has been incorporated before adding the next. When 1 tablespoon has been added, begin to add the oil a few drops at a time. When about ¼ cup of the oil has been added and the emulsion has taken—the mixture will have thickened and become homogenous—add the next ¼ cup by teaspoonfuls, making sure that each is incorporated before adding more. Add the remaining oil in a thin, continuous stream, stopping occasionally to make sure all has been incorporated before adding more. Cover and refrigerate until needed.

Lemon Mayonnaise

MAKES ABOUT ½ CUP (enough for two tarts)

½ cup Basic Mayonnaise (recipe precedes)

1 tablespoon fresh lemon juice

Place the mayonnaise in a small bowl. Using a whisk or a fork, beat the lemon juice into the mayonnaise a few drops at a time until the mixture is smooth.

Oriental Sesame Mayonnaise

MAKES ABOUT ½ CUP (enough for two tarts)

½ cup Basic Mayonnaise (recipe precedes)

1 tablespoon Oriental sesame oil

Place the mayonnaise in a small bowl. Using a whisk or a fork, beat the sesame oil into the mayonnaise a few drops at a time until the mixture is smooth.

The Vegetables

In a large, heavy saucepan placed over moderately high heat, combine 2 quarts of water and 1 tablespoon of salt. When the water boils, drop the vegetables, one variety at a time, into the water and cook according to the chart below. (Some vegetables, depending on their age or tenderness, may require more or less cooking time, so occasionally taste one for doneness as they cook.) As each is done, remove with a slotted spoon and refresh under cold water; drain well.

> Broccoli flowerets, 2 inches long ..... 3-5 minutes
> Red or green bell pepper strips,
>   ¼ inch by 2¼ inches .... 3-5 minutes
> Small carrot slices, ¼ inch thick ..... 5-8 minutes
> Green peas .... 4-5 minutes
> Chinese snow peas .... 4 minutes

Glaze

MAKES ABOUT ¾ CUP

2 level teaspoons firmly packed cornstarch

¾ cup degreased chicken stock or broth, cold or at room temperature

1. Place the cornstarch in a small, heavy saucepan and stir in the stock with a fork or a whisk. Cook over moderate heat, stirring constantly, until the mixture comes to a full boil.

2. Remove the pan from the heat and immediately spoon the glaze over the assembled vegetable tarts. The glaze will set slightly as the tarts chill.

Lovely Layered Cheeses

(Photograph on page 95)

This innovative assortment of layered cheese loaves can be the focal point of any party table, yet the loaves are easy to put together. Beginning with a base of store-bought cream cheese, they are brightened with bits and pieces of vegetables, herbs, nuts, and meats. There is no cooking involved. Making them is simply a matter of layering one variety of cheese on top of another to create tasty combinations, beautiful patterns. Layered cheese loaves must, however, be completed the day before serving in order to give them enough time to firm in the refrigerator.

Here are three of my favorite layered creations. The first begins with a cream-cheese and basil blend, which is layered with zesty Provolone and mellow mozzarella and studded with Italian *pignoli* (pine nuts). The second starts with a nippy black olive and cream-cheese combination, which is topped with Gruyère and triple-crème cheeses and dotted with scallions, pimientos, and poppy seeds. The third loaf consists of mustard- and tomato-flavored cream-cheese layers, plus slices of smoked ham and Swiss cheese. Finally, the loaf is rolled in toasted sesame seeds.

Variations on this theme are virtually limitless, so, by all means, feel free to use your imagination to create personal designs and combinations.

Olive-Cheese and Scallion Loaf
MAKES ONE 1½-POUND LOAF

Olive Cream-Cheese Filling:
  8 ounces cream cheese, at room temperature
  ¼ pound Greek calamata *olives*, pitted (½ cup)

Layers:
  1 teaspoon olive oil
  10 ounces Gruyère cheese, sliced ⅛ inch thick

8 ounces triple-crème cheese, such as Explorateur, at room temperature
8 to 10 scallion greens
3 to 4 ounces whole pimientos, rinsed, dried, and cut into ¼-inch-wide strips

Coating:
  ¼ cup poppy seeds

1. Prepare the Olive Cream-Cheese Filling: Place the cream cheese in a bowl and beat until light and fluffy. Finely chop the olives and stir them into the cream cheese.

2. Layer the loaf pan: Brush a 3-cup loaf pan (7½ by 4 by 2¼ inches) with ½ teaspoon of the oil. Line the pan with plastic wrap, leaving a 1-inch overhang all around; brush the plastic wrap with the remaining ½ teaspoon oil.

3. Using the back of a spoon, evenly spread ⅓ cup of the olive cheese over the bottom of the pan. The first layer will slide a bit on the oil, so be patient and continue working the mixture until it is level. Trim one to two slices of the

Gruyère to fit the pan in a single layer and place it or them over the olive cheese. Spread the Gruyère with about 3 tablespoons of the triple-crème cheese. Arrange the scallion greens lengthwise, pressing them gently into the cheese. Carefully spread about 2 more tablespoons of the triple-crème cheese over the scallions just to cover.

4. Trim enough Gruyère slices to fit the pan in a single layer and place over the triple-crème cheese. Spread ¼ cup of the olive cheese over the Gruyère. Add another layer of Gruyère trimmed to fit and spread with 3 tablespoons of the triple-crème cheese.

5. Arrange the pimiento strips lengthwise in rows spaced ¼ inch apart, pressing them gently into the cheese. Carefully spread the remaining 3 to 4 tablespoons triple-crème cheese over the pimientos. Cover with another layer of Gruyère cheese trimmed to fit the pan.

6. Spread the remaining (about ½ cup) olive cheese over the Gruyère. Trim the remaining Gruyère to fit the pan in a single layer and place it over the olive cheese.

7. Cover the cheese loaf with plastic wrap and refrigerate for 12 hours or overnight. To unmold, invert the pan and tap the edges on your work surface. If the cheese does not unmold, gently pull it out with the ends of the plastic wrap; remove the plastic wrap.

8. Coat the loaf: Place the poppy seeds on a baking sheet or plate and carefully roll the loaf in the seeds to coat the sides and top. Serve slightly chilled.

Basil and Provolone Loaf
MAKES ONE 1½-POUND LOAF

Basil Cream-Cheese Filling:
12 ounces cream cheese, at room
   temperature
¼ cup freshly grated Parmesan
   cheese
1 tablespoon crushed, minced garlic
1½ teaspoons dried basil, crumbled
½ teaspoon salt
¼ teaspoon freshly ground pepper

Layers:
1 teaspoon olive oil
6 slices (each ⅛ inch thick)
   Provolone cheese (about 6 ounces)
½ cup (3 ounces) pine nuts
   (pignoli)
12 ounces mozzarella cheese, sliced
   ¼ inch thick

1. Prepare the Basil Cream-Cheese Filling: Place the cream cheese in a bowl and beat it until light and fluffy. Add the Parmesan cheese, garlic, basil, salt, and pepper and blend well.

2. Layer the loaf pan: Brush a 3-cup loaf pan (7½ by 4 by 2¼ inches) with ½ teaspoon of the oil. Line the pan with plastic wrap, leaving a 1-inch overhang all around; brush the plastic wrap with the remaining ½ teaspoon oil.

3. Using the back of a spoon, evenly spread ¼ cup of the basil cheese over the bottom of the pan. The first layer will slide a bit on the oil, so be patient and continue to spread until it is level. Trim two slices of the Provolone to fit the pan in a single layer and place them over the basil cheese.

4. Spread the Provolone with ¼ cup of the basil cheese. Arrange ¼ cup of the pine nuts over the cheese in evenly spaced lengthwise rows, pressing them gently into the cheese. Carefully spread about 2 tablespoons basil cheese over the nuts just to cover.

5. Trim half the mozzarella slices to fit the pan in a single layer and cover the basil cheese with them. Spread the mozzarella with about 2 tablespoons of the basil cheese. Trim two more slices of the Provolone to fit the pan and arrange them over the basil cheese.

6. Spread the Provolone with about 2 tablespoons of the basil cheese. Arrange the remaining ¼ cup of pine nuts in evenly spaced lengthwise rows, pressing them gently into the cheese. Carefully spread about 2 tablespoons basil cheese over the nuts just to cover.

7. Trim the remaining slices of mozzarella to fit the pan in a single layer and place them over the basil cheese. Spread the mozzarella with half the remaining basil cheese and top it with the remaining two slices of Provolone trimmed to fit the pan. Wrap and refrigerate the remaining basil cheese.

8. Cover the cheese loaf with plastic wrap and refrigerate for 12 hours or overnight. One hour before unmolding the loaf, remove the remaining basil cheese from the refrigerator and let it come to room temperature. To unmold the loaf, invert the pan and tap the edges on your work surface. If the loaf does not unmold, gently pull it out with the ends of the plastic wrap. Remove the plastic wrap and evenly spread the basil cheese over the sides of the loaf. Serve slightly chilled.

Mustard-Cheese and Ham Loaf
MAKES ONE 2-POUND LOAF

Tomato Cream-Cheese Filling:
12 ounces cream cheese, at room temperature
3 tablespoons tomato paste
½ teaspoon salt
¼ teaspoon freshly ground pepper

Mustard Cream-Cheese Filling:
8 ounces cream cheese, softened
1 tablespoon plus 1 teaspoon powdered mustard
1 tablespoon plus 1 teaspoon Dijon-style mustard
¼ teaspoon salt

Layers:
1 teaspoon olive oil
14 ounces Swiss cheese, sliced ⅛ inch thick
8 ounces cooked ham, cut into ¼- by ¼- by 2-inch julienne strips

Coating:
¼ cup sesame seeds

1. **Prepare the Tomato Cream-Cheese Filling:** Place the cream cheese in a bowl and beat it until light and fluffy. Blend in the tomato paste, salt, and pepper.

2. **Prepare the Mustard Cream-Cheese Filling:** Place the cream cheese in a bowl and beat it until light and fluffy. Blend in the powdered and prepared mustards and salt.

3. **Layer the loaf pan:** Brush a 4-cup loaf pan (8 by 4 by 2½ inches) with ½ teaspoon of the olive oil. Line the pan with plastic wrap, leaving a 1-inch overhang all around. Brush the plastic wrap with the remaining olive oil.

4. Using the back of a spoon, evenly spread ½ cup of the tomato cheese over the bottom of the pan. The first layer will slide a bit on the oil, so be patient and work the mixture until it is level. Trim enough slices of the Swiss cheese to fit the pan in a single layer and place them on top of the tomato cheese. Spread ½ cup of the mustard cheese evenly over the Swiss. Arrange a layer of half of the ham strips lengthwise in evenly spaced rows, pressing them gently into the cheese. Carefully spread 2 to 3 tablespoons of mustard cheese over the ham just to cover.

5. Trim enough slices of Swiss cheese to fit the pan in a single layer and place over the mustard cheese. Spread ¼ cup of the tomato cheese over the Swiss slices.

6. Spread ¼ cup of tomato cheese over the Swiss and top it with another layer of Swiss slices trimmed to fit. Spread ¼ cup mustard cheese over the Swiss and arrange the remaining strips of ham in lengthwise rows, pressing them into the cheese. Carefully spread the remaining mustard cheese (about 2 tablespoons) over the ham and top it with a layer of Swiss slices trimmed to fit.

7. Spread ¼ cup of tomato cheese in the pan and top with Swiss slices trimmed to fit. Spread the remaining tomato cheese over the Swiss and top it with a single layer of the remaining Swiss trimmed to fit.

8. Cover the cheese loaf with plastic wrap and refrigerate 12 hours or overnight. To unmold, invert the pan and tap the edges on your work surface. If the loaf does not unmold, gently pull it out with the ends of the plastic wrap; remove the plastic wrap.

9. Coat the loaf: In a small, ungreased skillet set over moderate heat, toast the sesame seeds, stirring, until they turn golden brown, about 3 minutes. Turn out onto a paper towel and let them cool; then place the seeds on a baking sheet or plate. Carefully roll the cheese loaf in the seeds to coat the sides and top. Serve slightly chilled.

Chilled Vegetable Lasagne with Creamy Tomato Sauce

Here is a recipe for cold lasagne that is probably very different from any you've ever tasted. During the warm-weather months, it makes a refreshing, cool pasta course when served before simple roast chicken, beef, or duck. You might also serve it with braised pork chops or a stuffed breast of veal. If you'd rather keep your menu vegetarian, serve the lasagne with buttered corn, sautéed zucchini, cabbage, or mushrooms, and, perhaps, stuffed baked onions.

The three colorful layers of filling—orange, white, and green—are made from flavorful blends of herbs, vegetables, and cheese spread between sheets of curly-edged lasagne noodles. The cool Creamy Tomato Sauce, to be spooned over or around the lasagne, provides additional contrast in flavor as well as in color. Both the sauce and the lasagne keep well in the refrigerator, so prepare them a day before you plan to serve them; you will find that the flavors are enhanced and that the lasagne slices more neatly.

Chilled Vegetable Lasagne

You will need fresh basil leaves to make this lasagne, so make sure that they are available before beginning. You will also need a 1½-quart loaf pan measuring 8½ by 4½ by 2¾ inches deep.

MAKES 14 SLICES, EACH ½ INCH THICK (or 14 pasta-course servings when an antipasto and main dish are served)

Basil-and-Cheese Filling:
- 2 cups (lightly packed) fresh basil leaves
- 3 tablespoons olive oil
- 2 large garlic cloves, chopped
- ¾ cup whole-milk ricotta cheese
- 1 egg
- ½ cup freshly grated Parmesan cheese
- ½ cup plain, dry bread crumbs
- ½ teaspoon salt
- ½ teaspoon freshly ground pepper

Ricotta-Cheese Filling:
- 1 cup whole-milk ricotta cheese
- ¼ cup freshly grated Parmesan cheese
- 1 egg
- 2 tablespoons plain, dry bread crumbs
- ½ teaspoon salt
- ½ teaspoon freshly ground pepper

Carrot-and-Lemon Filling:
- 4 to 5 medium-size carrots (8 ounces), trimmed and cut into slices ½ inch thick
- 1 egg
- 3 tablespoons fresh lemon juice
- 2 tablespoons olive oil
- ½ cup whole-milk ricotta cheese
- ⅓ cup plain, dry bread crumbs
- ¼ cup freshly grated Parmesan cheese
- 1½ teaspoons sugar
- ½ teaspoon salt
- ½ teaspoon freshly ground pepper

Assembly:
- 2 teaspoons salt
- 4 tablespoons olive oil
- 10 curly-edged lasagne noodles (8 ounces)
- ¼ cup freshly grated Parmesan cheese

Garnish:
- 2 cups Creamy Tomato Sauce (recipe follows)
- 1 medium-size to large carrot tiny basil leaves

1. Prepare the Basil-and-Cheese Filling: Place the basil leaves in a food processor or blender along with the 3 tablespoons olive oil, garlic, ricotta, and the egg; purée, scraping down the sides of the container with a spatula as necessary. If using a food processor, add the Parmesan, bread crumbs, salt, and pepper and process until well blended. If using a blender, transfer the contents to a medium-size bowl and stir in the Parmesan, bread crumbs, salt, and pepper until blended. You should have 1¾ cups. Cover and set aside.

2. Prepare the Ricotta-Cheese Filling: In a medium-size bowl, beat together the ricotta, Parmesan, and egg until blended. Stir in the bread crumbs, salt, and pepper. Cover and set aside.

3. Prepare the Carrot-and-Lemon Filling: Bring a medium-size pot of water to a boil and drop in the carrots. When the boiling resumes, cook over moderate heat, partially covered, until the carrots are tender, 8 to 10 minutes. Drain and rinse under cold running water; set aside to cool to room temperature.

4. Place the carrots in a food processor or blender along with the egg, lemon juice, and the 2 tablespoons olive oil. If using a processor, add the ricotta, bread crumbs, Parmesan, sugar, salt, and pepper and process until blended, scraping down the sides with a spatula as necessary. If using a blender, transfer the contents to a medium-size bowl and stir in the ricotta, bread crumbs, Parmesan, sugar, salt, and pepper until blended; you should have 1⅔ cups. Cover and set aside.

5. Assembly: Bring a large, heavy (preferably nonstick) pot of water, with the 2 teaspoons salt, to a boil over high heat. Meanwhile, preheat the oven to 375°F.

6. Brush a 1½-quart, 8½- by 4½- by 2¾-inch loaf pan with ½ tablespoon of the olive oil. Cut a strip of aluminum foil that is the width of the loaf pan with enough additional length to overhang the two ends of the pan by 3 inches (see

ILLUSTRATION A-1

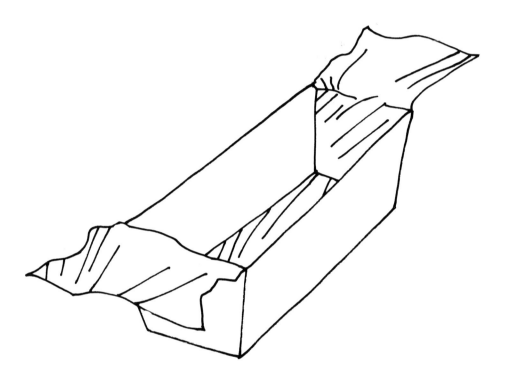

illus. A-1). Brush the foil with ½ tablespoon of the remaining olive oil. Set the pan aside until needed.

7. When the water is boiling rapidly, add the lasagne noodles one at a time. Stir gently with a long-handled, slotted spoon until the boiling resumes. Stirring gently but frequently, boil over moderately high heat for 8 minutes, or until the noodles have softened but are still firm to the bite. Drain the noodles, rinse under cold water, and lay them out flat in a single layer on paper towels. Cool to room temperature.

8. Lay four of the lasagne noodles lengthwise across the bottom of the prepared pan in an overlapping arrangement (see illus. A-2), with the ends of the noodles extending 3 inches over each end of the loaf pan. Spread all the Basil-and-Cheese Filling over the bottom of the noodle-lined pan and fold the ends of the pasta inward over it.

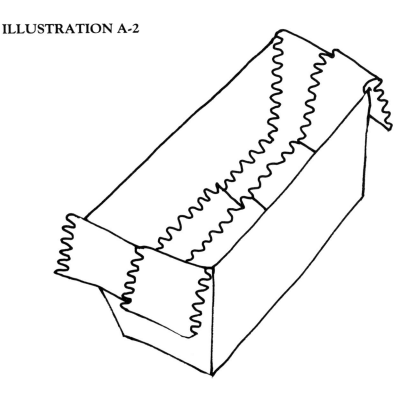

9. Brush the pasta with 1 tablespoon of the remaining olive oil and spread the Ricotta-Cheese Filling over the layer you just made. Top the layer with four overlapping lasagne noodles as you did at the beginning of step 8, with the ends extending 3 inches over the pan ends. Spread with the Carrot-and-Lemon Filling.

10. Trim the two remaining lasagne noodles to fit neatly and flat on top of the filling (the pan should be packed full at this point), brush the noodles with 1 tablespoon of the remaining olive oil, and then sprinkle with the Parmesan. Fold the extending ends of the lasagne noodles inward over the cheese and brush with the remaining 1 tablespoon olive oil. Fold the 3-inch aluminum-foil extensions downward snugly against the outside of the loaf pan. Wrap the pan tightly in two layers of heavy-duty aluminum foil and place it in a 13- by 9-inch baking pan. Fill the baking pan halfway with hot water. Bake for 1 hour. Remove from the oven and let cool to room temperature. Wipe the outside of the foil dry and refrigerate overnight before unwrapping.

ILLUSTRATION B-1

ILLUSTRATION B-2

11. Meanwhile, prepare the Creamy Tomato Sauce and refrigerate it until cold or overnight.

12. To serve, unwrap the chilled loaf of lasagne and run a knife along the two long sides of the pan to loosen the edges. Invert the pan onto a serving platter; remove the pan and the aluminum-foil lining. Slice away the two ends to make them even. Cut the loaf into slices about ½ inch thick and transfer them to small individual plates. Let them rest, along with the sauce, for about 10 minutes to take the chill off. Then either nap about 2 tablespoons of the sauce directly over each end of the slice or pour it directly onto the plate, placing half next to the carrot layer and the other half next to the basil layer.

13. To make carrot flowers: Peel the carrot for garnish and cut off a 2-inch length (see illus. B-1). Using a paring knife, cut out triangular wedges the length

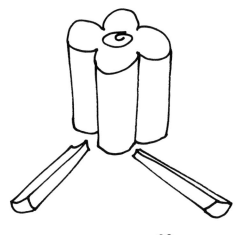

33

of the carrot (see illus. B-2). Lay the carrot on its side and slice horizontally to form flowers (see illus. B-3). Decorate each plate with a carrot flower, a triangular carrot wedge for a stem, and some basil leaves (see illus. B-4).

ILLUSTRATION B-4

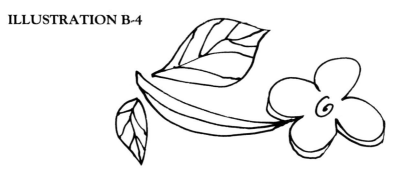

Creamy Tomato Sauce

This sauce calls for canned, imported tomatoes because the fresh ones usually available these days in the United States are pulpy and pink, having been designed to withstand shipping and a long shelf life rather than for flavor. You will need cheesecloth for making the bouquet garni, *which is used to flavor the sauce.*

MAKES ABOUT 2 CUPS

1 *parsley sprig*
1 *bay leaf*
3 *tablespoons chopped fresh basil leaves*
½ *teaspoon dried oregano (or 1 teaspoon fresh)*

8 *peppercorns*
1 *can (35 ounces) Italian peeled tomatoes*
1 *teaspoon sugar*
1 *cup heavy cream salt to taste*

1. Make the *bouquet garni:* Place the parsley, bay leaf, basil, oregano, and peppercorns for the *bouquet garni* in the center of an 8-inch square of several layers of cheesecloth; gather it up into a pouch and tie securely with string. Trim away and discard the excess cheesecloth; set aside.

2. Place the tomatoes and their liquid into a wire sieve set over a heavy, medium-size, noncorrosive saucepan. To remove the seeds and purée the tomatoes, rapidly whisk the tomatoes and juice around the sieve, pressing against the sieve as you whisk. Before discarding the seeds, scrape any tomato purée clinging to the underside of the sieve into the pan.

3. Place the *bouquet garni* into the tomatoes along with the sugar and heavy cream and bring to a boil over moderately high heat; reduce the heat slightly and boil, stirring occasionally, until reduced to 2 cups, 20 to 30 minutes. Each time that you stir, press the spoon against the *bouquet garni* to help release the flavor. Add salt to taste, remove from the heat, and transfer to a small bowl; immediately cover with plastic wrap placed directly on the surface of the sauce. Cool to room temperature and then refrigerate until well chilled, preferably overnight. If any of the seeds are still in the sauce or if it seems lumpy, strain again. Taste for seasoning—if it is too acidic, add a little sugar; if too sweet, add a little salt. Let rest at room temperature for 10 minutes before serving.

Salade Chinoise
(Photograph on page 2)

Here, a dramatic warm salad with an Oriental influence offers a welcome and colorful change from the ordinary salad of assorted chilled greens. To create it, rings of crisp watercress, marinated bean sprouts, and lightly stir-fried snow peas are formed into a nest to present a Chinese-seasoned chicken salad that includes mushrooms, celery, and scallions. It is a convenient salad to make because all the preparation can be done ahead of time, leaving only a few minutes of stir-frying to be done at serving time. It makes an impressive, flavorful way to begin an elegant dinner.

Salade Chinoise
SERVES 6

Marinated Bean Sprouts:
- 1 pound fresh bean sprouts
- 2 tablespoons Oriental sesame oil
- 1 tablespoon soy sauce
- 2 tablespoons rice vinegar

Dressing:
- ¼ cup peanut oil
- 1 tablespoon Oriental sesame oil
- 2 tablespoons minced fresh gingerroot
- 1 teaspoon minced garlic
- 2 tablespoons rice vinegar
- 1 tablespoon soy sauce

Chicken Salad:
- ¼ pound Chinese snow peas, trimmed and cut lengthwise into ⅛-inch-wide strips

- 3 cups shredded, cooked chicken-breast meat (2 whole breasts)
- 2 ribs celery, thinly sliced on the bias (1 cup)
- 6 large mushrooms, thinly sliced
- ½ cup thinly sliced scallions
- 3 tablespoons rice vinegar
- 1 tablespoon soy sauce
- 1 tablespoon Oriental sesame oil

Garnishes:
- 2 bunches watercress, washed, dried, and large stems removed
- 2 tablespoons toasted sesame seeds (see Note)
- 2 roasted, peeled red bell peppers or pimientos

Note: Toast sesame seeds in a small skillet set over low heat, stirring, until the seeds are golden brown.

1. Marinate the bean sprouts: Bring a large kettle of water to a full boil and drop in the bean sprouts; let them rest in the water for 1 minute and then drain them in a colander. Rinse under cold running water and drain on paper towels.

Place the bean sprouts in a large mixing bowl and add the sesame oil, soy sauce, and rice vinegar; toss gently. Let the bean sprouts marinate at room temperature while you prepare the dressing and chicken salad.

2. Prepare the dressing: Combine all the dressing ingredients in a blender and process at medium speed until the garlic and gingerroot are pulverized (or grind the garlic and gingerroot in a mortar with a pestle and stir in the remaining dressing ingredients).

3. Prepare the chicken salad: Heat the dressing in a wok or a large, heavy skillet until very hot but not smoking. Add the snow peas and stir-fry for 1 minute; remove half of them with a slotted spoon and reserve. Add the shredded chicken to the snow peas remaining in the wok or skillet and stir-fry for 1 minute. Add the celery and stir-fry another minute. Remove the wok or skillet from the heat and stir in the mushrooms, scallions, vinegar, soy sauce, and sesame oil; toss gently.

4. Assemble the salad: Referring to the photograph, arrange the watercress around the edge of a 10- or 12-inch platter. Drain the bean sprouts and form them into a nest inside the watercress ring. Arrange the reserved snow peas in a ring inside the bean-sprout nest and mound the chicken salad in the center. Sprinkle with the sesame seeds. Cut the red peppers or pimientos into seven triangles, each about 3 inches long, and arrange them into a sunburst design on top of the chicken salad. Serve warm.

2 Breads

Bas-Relief Oat Bread

(Photograph on page 89)

A big, round, crusty loaf of bread with a three-dimensional design of grapes and leaves is easy to make, very beautiful, and very delicious. Freshly baked bread has many roles that it can play. It can be the center of attraction at a wine- and cheese-tasting party or an earthy addition to a dinner party or buffet. Since this hearty oat bread can also cause one to conjure up thoughts of a bountiful autumn harvest feast, you might invent some of your own bread shapes to carry out this theme, such as a sheaf of wheat, acorn-shaped rolls, and cornbread sticks shaped like ears of corn.

Bas-Relief Oat Bread

A small portion of the dough for this crusty oat bread is reserved to make a three-dimensional design of grapes and leaves to top the loaf. Sifting flour over the bread before baking it adds a professional quality that enhances the bas-relief design. To bake the bread, you will need a heavy baking sheet at least 12 inches wide. You will also need to cut two leaf patterns (instructions follow).

MAKES ONE 12-INCH-ROUND LOAF

2 cups milk
3 cups old-fashioned rolled oats
⅔ cup vegetable shortening
2 tablespoons salt
½ cup sugar
1½ cups warm water (105°F. to 115°F.)

2 envelopes (¼ ounce each) active dry yeast
7 to 9 cups sifted all-purpose flour
2 eggs, at room temperature

1. Place the milk in a medium-size saucepan over low heat and scald it; it should come just to a simmer but not boil. Meanwhile, in a large, heatproof bowl, combine the oats, shortening, and salt; pour the hot milk over the oat mixture. Place 2 teaspoons of the sugar in a small bowl and set aside. Add the remaining sugar to the oat mixture, stirring to dissolve. Let rest for 5 minutes, stirring once or twice.

2. Meanwhile, pour ½ cup of the warm water over the sugar in the small bowl; sprinkle the yeast over the water and stir to dissolve. Let the yeast proof until foamy, 5 to 10 minutes.

3. Check the temperature of the remaining 1 cup warm water; it should be about 110°F. Add it to the oat mixture, beat in 1 cup of the flour, the eggs, and the yeast. Gradually add enough of the remaining flour (reserve 2 tablespoons for decoration) to make a moderately stiff dough. Knead the dough on a lightly floured surface, kneading in more flour if necessary to prevent the dough from sticking, until it is very smooth and elastic, about 10 minutes. Let the dough rest for 5 minutes.

4. Fill a large bowl with hot tap water. When the bowl is warm, discard the water and thoroughly dry the bowl. Lightly oil the bowl and add the dough, turning it once to coat the top. Cover the bowl and let the dough rise in a warm, draft-free place (a turned-off oven with a pilot light is ideal) until doubled in bulk, 1 to 1½ hours.

5. Punch the dough down with your fist, knead it for 1 minute, and let it rest, covered, for 10 minutes. Lightly oil a baking sheet that is at least 12 inches wide. Remove about 1 cup of the dough for decoration, cover it, and set it aside. Shape the remaining dough into a smooth, round loaf about 8 inches in diameter and place it on the prepared baking sheet. Loosely cover the loaf while you prepare the decorations.

6. On a lightly floured surface, pat out half the dough reserved for decorations to about a ¼-inch thickness or slightly less. Using the two leaf patterns, cut out one large leaf and two small ones. Gather the scraps and combine them with the remaining dough. Uncover the large dough round, paint the backs of the dough leaves with water, and, referring to illustration A for placement, attach them to the bread. To form the grapes, make a number of small balls with the reserved dough by rolling pieces between the palms of your hands, making some about ¾ inch in diameter and others about 1 inch. Again referring to the illustration, arrange them in a cluster, placing some of the grapes on top of others and attaching them with water. For tendrils, roll out five thin strands of dough and attach them to the loaf with water, coiling the ends as shown in the illustration. Cover the bread and let it rise in a warm, draft-free place until doubled in bulk, about 45 minutes.

ILLUSTRATION A

7. When the dough has almost doubled in bulk, preheat the oven to 375°F. Uncover the bread. Holding a strainer in one hand and 2 tablespoons of reserved flour in the other, sprinkle the flour into the strainer as you shake the strainer back and forth over the dough, continuing until the loaf is lightly coated all over.

8. Bake the loaf in the center of the oven for about 1 hour, or until the bottom sounds hollow when tapped. Transfer to a rack and cool before serving.

Leaf Patterns

Using tracing paper and a pencil, trace over the two following leaf patterns. Using scissors, cut out the patterns and then trace around them on lightweight cardboard; cut them out. Use as patterns for making the leaves from dough.

LEAF PATTERNS

Sausage *Palmiers*

almiers, the classic French pastries named after the palm tree, are traditionally made from puff pastry and sugar, and they take a full day to prepare from scratch. Here, however, the technique has become the inspiration for a fast-and-savory version. A quick butter-and-basil dough is stirred up, rolled out, and spread with a delicious, aromatic Italian Sausage and Chicken Filling. After the dough has been rolled up from opposite ends to enclose the filling, it is then sliced and baked. The resulting double-swirled Sausage *Palmiers* make an extraordinary addition to a brunch, but they are also tasteful complements to soups and salads.

You can prepare the filling for this recipe a day before you need it and then keep it, covered, in the refrigerator. Before spreading it over the dough, let it soften to room temperature. Or, several hours ahead, you can prepare the entire double-roll, cover it, and keep it refrigerated until serving time.

Italian Sausage and Chicken Filling

You will need a meat grinder or food processor to make this recipe.
MAKES ABOUT 2 CUPS

¾ pound sweet Italian sausage with
    fennel seeds (about 6 small links)
2 garlic cloves, minced
1 whole, skinless, boneless chicken
    breast (8 ounces)

⅓ cup heavy cream
¼ cup tomato paste
½ teaspoon freshly ground pepper

1. Remove the casings from the sausage links and crumble the meat into a heavy, medium-size skillet. Stirring to break up the pieces of meat, cook over moderate heat for 5 minutes and then add the garlic. Continue cooking until the sausage is cooked through, about 2 to 3 minutes longer. Using a slotted spoon, transfer the mixture to a bowl, leaving the drippings in the pan, and cool the sausage to room temperature.

2. Cut the chicken breast in half lengthwise and add the halves to the drippings in the skillet. Sauté over moderate heat, turning them several times, until cooked through, about 10 minutes—the flesh in the center should be firm and no longer pink. Remove the pieces with a slotted spoon and cool to room temperature.

3. Cut the chicken into 1-inch pieces. If you are using a meat grinder, put the sausage mixture and the chicken through the fine blade; repeat once more. Place the meat in a medium-size bowl and stir in the cream, tomato paste, and pepper. If using a food processor, simply combine all the ingredients in the container and purée.

Sausage *Palmiers*
MAKES 24

3 cups all-purpose flour
2 tablespoons plus 2 teaspoons
    baking powder
2 teaspoons dried basil leaves,
    crumbled
¼ teaspoon salt
¾ cup (1½ sticks) unsalted butter,
    chilled and cut into thin slices

1 cup milk
2 tablespoons unsalted butter,
    softened to room temperature
2 cups Italian Sausage and Chicken
    Filling, at room temperature
    (recipe precedes)
½ cup grated Parmesan cheese

1. Prepare the dough: Preheat the oven to 400°F. and lightly oil one or two
baking sheets. In a large mixing bowl, combine the flour, baking powder, basil,
and salt. Using a pastry blender or two knives, cut in the chilled butter until the
mixture resembles coarse meal. Pour the milk over the mixture and quickly stir
with a fork just until the dough can be gathered into a ball. On a generously
floured work surface, pat the dough out, turning it several times, to a rectangle
that measures 9 by 12 inches. Spread the softened butter over two-thirds of the

ILLUSTRATION A

 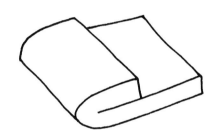 

dough (see illus. A). Fold the unbuttered third of the dough over half of the
buttered dough and then fold it over once more—you will have three layers of
dough separated by two layers of butter. Using additional flour on your work
surface if necessary to prevent the dough from sticking, working with a lightly
floured rolling pin, and turning the dough occasionally, roll the dough out in
both directions to a 15-inch square.

2. Drop the filling by spoonfuls over the dough, and using a spatula or your
fingers, spread it evenly over all, leaving a 1-inch border along two opposite
edges. Sprinkle the filling evenly with ¼ cup of the Parmesan cheese. Beginning
with one of the border ends, roll up the dough to the center point to enclose the
filling; do the same from the other border end (see illus. B). When the two ends

ILLUSTRATION B

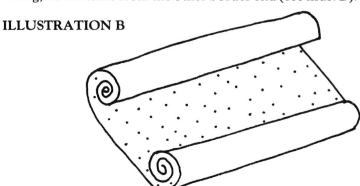

ILLUSTRATION C

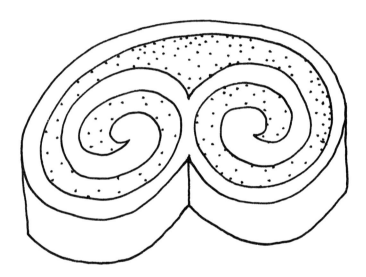

meet in the center (see illus. C), brush the seam with water and push the two rolls together so that they adhere.

3. Using a sharp knife, cut the filled dough into slices about ⅝ inch thick and place them on the prepared baking sheet(s) (see illus. D), leaving about 1 inch of

ILLUSTRATION D

space between them and reshaping them if necessary. Using the remaining ¼ cup of Parmesan cheese, sprinkle ½ teaspoon over each *palmier*. Bake for about 15 minutes, or until puffed and slightly golden. Serve hot or warm. If you have any leftovers, wrap them tightly and refrigerate overnight. To reheat chilled *palmiers*, preheat the oven to 350°F., place the *palmiers* in a single layer on a large sheet of aluminum foil, wrap them tightly, and bake for about 15 minutes or until hot.

Roast-Beef and Spinach Sandwich Loaf

To make this robust luncheon loaf, a long, unsliced Pullman loaf of bread is split horizontally into three layers and spread with a layer of Roast-Beef Filling flavored with horseradish and pickles and another of Spinach Filling spiked with mustard, garlic, and scallions. After filling and chilling, the savory loaf is "frosted" with cream cheese and decorated with Tomato Roses and tender, baby celery leaves.

These decorated loaves were once very popular fare for luncheons, teas, and bridge-club gatherings. Perhaps it was when bakers began to tint the loaves of bread for them pink and green that their popularity waned. After the cook at home had filled them with the ubiquitous yellow egg salad, one wasn't sure whether he or she were about to bite into a cake or a confection of pastel Easter colors or, indeed, really a sandwich. Thank goodness, those days are long gone—now one can begin the project with a loaf of natural whole-wheat bread or a good, hearty white bread.

A Pullman loaf of bread is fun to use for this recipe because it is longer than a standard loaf of bread, which makes it more dramatic; it can also serve more people. (The Pullman loaf, by the way, was so named because its long, rectangular shape resembled that of the Pullman passenger car of a train.) If you cannot find a Pullman loaf of bread, you can improvise by trimming the crusts away of two regular-size, unsliced bread loaves and putting the two loaves together. After coating them with the cream cheese, the joining will be invisible. You can also use just one regular-size loaf of bread, but there will be some filling left—use it to make delicious lunchbox sandwiches.

Roast-Beef and Spinach Sandwich Loaf

If you prefer a vegetarian loaf, omit the Roast-Beef Filling and double the recipe for the Spinach Filling. Note that a total of three 8-ounce packages of cream cheese is enough to make this recipe—2 ounces in the Roast-Beef Filling, two packages to frost the loaf, and 6 ounces to pipe the shell borders.

MAKES ABOUT 16 SERVINGS (or 8 servings if using a regular-size loaf)

1 unsliced Pullman loaf of bread (white or whole wheat), about 4 by 4 by 13 inches, or one or two regular-size unsliced loaves of bread, each about 4 by 4 by 8 inches

4 tablespoons mayonnaise (8 teaspoons if using one regular-size loaf)

1⅓ cups Roast-Beef Filling (recipe follows)

1⅓ cups Fresh Spinach Filling (recipe follows)

8 tablespoons (1 stick) unsalted butter (4 tablespoons if using a regular-size loaf), at room temperature

2 packages (8 ounces each) cream cheese (one 8-ounce package if using one regular-size loaf), plus 6 ounces for piping border, at room temperature

Garnish:

3 Tomato Roses, made from one large and two medium-size tomatoes (instructions follow) celery leaves

1. Using a long, serrated knife, evenly trim away the crust from all four sides and the top of the bread loaf to make a rectangular shape; leave the bottom crust intact. Using toothpicks if necessary as a guide, slice the loaf horizontally into three even layers. Place the bottom layer, crust side down, on a long, rectangular serving tray or wooden cutting board (make sure that it will fit into your refrigerator). Keep the remaining two layers in the order in which they were cut and cover them.

2. Spread the top of the bread on the tray with 1 tablespoon of the mayonnaise (if using a regular-size loaf, spread with 2 teaspoons). Spread the Roast-Beef Filling evenly over the coated bread (if using a regular-size loaf, spread the filling so that it is about ½ inch thick), making sure that the edge of the filling is even with the edge of the bread all around.

3. Using the middle layer of bread, spread the bottom with 1 tablespoon mayonnaise (2 teaspoons if using a regular-size loaf) and place it, mayonnaise side down, over the beef filling. Spread the top of the bread with 1 tablespoon of mayonnaise (2 teaspoons if using a regular-size loaf). Spread the Fresh Spinach Filling evenly over the coated bread (if using a regular-size loaf, spread the filling so that it is about ½ inch thick), making sure that the filling is even with the edge of the bread all around. Spread the bottom of the top bread layer with the remaining 1 tablespoon mayonnaise (remaining 2 teaspoons if using a regular-size loaf) and place it, mayonnaise side down, over the filling.

4. Use enough of the softened butter to spread the sides and top of the loaf with a thin coating. Refrigerate until the butter has set. Cover the loaf loosely with a damp linen towel or aluminum foil and refrigerate until the filling is cold, about 2 hours.

5. Two to six hours before you wish to serve or display the loaf on your table, remove the tray from the refrigerator and, using a spatula, spread a smooth, even layer of cream cheese over the sides and top of the loaf so that the coating is about ⅛ inch thick. If you want to pipe a shell border around the edge (see illus. A), fit a pastry bag with a star tip about ¼ inch wide and place 6 ounces of

ILLUSTRATION A

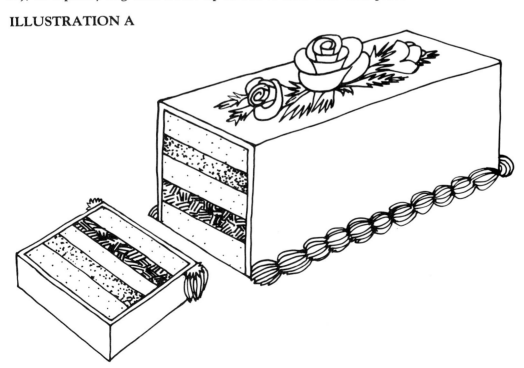

softened cream cheese into the bag. To make the shell border (practice on waxed paper first—you can reuse the cheese), hold the bag at a 45-degree angle with your right hand and use your left index finger to guide and steady the point as you move it. Squeeze out a shell shape, lifting the tip about ⅛ inch up from the waxed paper and applying more pressure as you squeeze out the widest part of the shell; to taper off the shell, stop squeezing and bring the point back down to the waxed paper. Overlapping the point of the shell, squeeze out another shell. Repeat the procedure all around the outside edge of the loaf. Refrigerate the loaf, uncovered, until the cream cheese has set. (If you would like to hold the loaf in the refrigerator for up to 6 hours before serving, cover it with a sheet of plastic wrap.) Meanwhile, make the Tomato Roses, cover, and refrigerate for up to several hours.

6. Remove the chilled sandwich loaf from the refrigerator and center the largest Tomato Rose on top. Referring to illustration A, add a few celery leaves and then add the two remaining roses, each facing outward from the center; garnish with more celery leaves if desired.

7. When ready to serve, use a long, serrated knife to cut the loaf into ¾-inch-thick slices. Using a spatula, carefully transfer each to a serving plate and let the slices sit at room temperature for 15 minutes or so to take the chill off. The loaf itself will hold at room temperature for as long as several hours.

Roast-Beef Filling

You can make this filling from leftover, well-done (rare won't work) roast beef, but tender braised brisket of beef is better because it shreds more easily, adding a welcome texture and flavor. If you are too rushed to cook a brisket yourself, ask your local delicatessen to cut a few ¼-inch-thick slices for you. If you do cook your own, begin the day before you want to make the filling.
MAKES ABOUT 1⅓ CUPS

6 ounces fully-cooked brisket of beef or roast beef, cut into ¼-inch dice (1 cup, tightly packed)
¼ cup mayonnaise
2 ounces cream cheese, at room temperature
3 tablespoons finely chopped sweet

pickle or well-drained sweet relish
1½ tablespoons (squeezed dry) prepared white horseradish
½ teaspoon freshly ground pepper
salt to taste
1 to 2 tablespoons sweet paprika if using whole-wheat bread

Place the beef in a medium-size mixing bowl along with the mayonnaise; using a fork, stir the mixture, breaking the beef into shreds by pressing the mixture against the side of bowl. Stir in the cream cheese, sweet pickle, horseradish, pepper, and salt to taste. If you are using whole-wheat bread, stir in the paprika. Cover and set aside at room temperature for up to 1 hour or refrigerate and then allow to come back to room temperature before using.

Fresh Spinach Filling
MAKES ABOUT 1⅓ CUPS

1 cup (squeezed dry and packed) cooked, chopped spinach leaves (1 pound to 1½ pounds, depending on number and thickness of stems)
1 tablespoon vegetable oil
2 garlic cloves, minced and crushed or put through a press
1 tablespoon Dijon-style mustard
2 tablespoons fresh lemon juice
¼ cup minced scallions with some of the green (about 4)
¼ teaspoon freshly grated nutmeg
½ teaspoon freshly ground pepper
3 tablespoons unsalted butter, at room temperature
2 hard-cooked egg yolks, sieved salt to taste

Place the spinach in a medium-size bowl and set aside. In a small, heavy skillet, combine the oil and garlic. Place it over low heat and cook gently for about 2 minutes, or until the garlic is softened but not beginning to turn golden. Pour the garlic and oil over the spinach. Stir in the mustard, lemon juice, scallions, nutmeg, pepper, butter, and egg yolks until well blended. Add salt to taste. Cover and set aside at room temperature for up to 1 hour or refrigerate and then allow to come back to room temperature before using.

Tomato Roses
To make three tomato roses, begin with one large tomato and two medium-size tomatoes. Starting at the bottom of one tomato (opposite the stem end; see illus. B-1) and using a paring knife, cut the peel along with about 1/16 inch of the

ILLUSTRATION B-1

flesh into a continuous strip about ¾ inch wide (see illus. B-2). Starting with the end (see illus. B-3) you first removed, roll the strip, skin side outward, into a

ILLUSTRATION B-2

ILLUSTRATION B-3

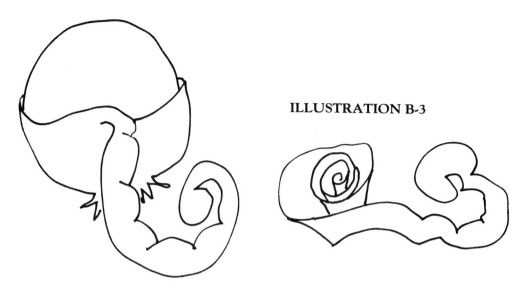

rose (see illus. B-4). Place it on a plate and repeat with the remaining two tomatoes. The resulting roses can be kept, covered with plastic or a damp paper towel, for about 2 hours. The results are perfect garnishes not only for this dish, but also for almost any main dish. Use the peeled tomatoes in a salad to accompany the meal.

ILLUSTRATION B-4

Bread Basket with Daisy Rolls

Bread can be shaped into many forms. You are probably already familiar with the long, thin loaves diagonally slashed across the top and the plump, round ones with designs radiating from the center. But breads can be made with much more specialized shapes. One bakery in Manhattan produces buns in the shape of turtles, and, for decades, our Mexican neighbors have been using bread dough to create such complicated forms as alligators, iguanas, and seashells.

This project results in a bread basket that has been woven over an upside-down bowl, using a fresh, puffy yeast dough. After glazing and baking, the basket is inverted and piled with golden daisy-shaped rolls, each with a center coated with crunchy poppy or sunflower seeds. *Voila*—an edible work of art that doubles as a centerpiece for a brunch, special lunch, or classic dinner.

Bread Basket with Daisy Rolls

(Photograph on page 96)

To make this unusual centerpiece, you will need an ovenproof bowl, preferably one of earthenware, but glass will also work. It should be about 8 inches in diameter and hold from 2 to 2½ quarts. It is also best to have three cookie sheets (baking sheets without edges), each about 15 by 12 inches. Be sure to work in a warm, draft-free kitchen whenever you bake bread.

MAKES ONE BASKET AND ABOUT 1½ DOZEN ROLLS

Dough:
- 3 cups milk
- ½ cup (1 stick) unsalted butter, sliced
- ⅓ cup sugar
- 2 teaspoons salt
- 3 envelopes (¼ ounce each) active dry yeast
- 11 to 12 cups all-purpose flour
- 5 eggs, at room temperature

Daisy Rolls:
- ¼ cup poppy seeds
- ¼ cup sunflower seeds

1. Prepare the dough: In a heavy, medium-size saucepan, combine the milk, butter, sugar, and salt over moderate heat. Stirring frequently, heat until the milk has scalded (bubbles will appear around the edge of the pan and the top of the milk will rise slightly). Transfer the mixture to a large, heatproof bowl (preferably heavy ceramic), place a thermometer into the liquid, and cool to 105°F. to 115°F. Sprinkle the yeast over the surface, stir the mixture until the yeast has dissolved, and then stir in 2 cups of the flour; whisk until smooth, cover, and let proof in a warm, draft-free place (85°F.) until almost doubled in bulk and foamy, about 20 minutes. If this does not happen, perhaps the liquid was too hot or cold or the yeast outdated; start again with fresh ingredients.

2. Whisk in four of the eggs, one at a time (reserve the fifth egg for glazing). Then stir in enough of the remaining flour to form a moderately stiff dough. (A total of 11 cups should be enough—use the remainder for dusting your work surface as you knead and shape the bread.) Knead the dough for 10 to 15 minutes, or until soft and smooth (if you are kneading it in a food processor or an electric dough kneader, work in batches and follow manufacturer's directions for the proper length of time). Place about 1 tablespoon of vegetable oil in a large, clean bowl; add the dough, turning it once to oil the top side. Cover and let rise in a warm (85°F.), draft-free place until doubled in bulk, 1 to 1½ hours.

3. Prepare the bread basket: Lightly oil two 15- by 12-inch cookie sheets. Lightly dust one with flour and tap off the excess. Center an 8-inch, 2- to 2½-quart ovenproof bowl upside down on the floured surface, and trace around it with your finger or the tip of a knife; set aside for step 7. Remove the bowl and place it, still upside down, on the oiled sheet without the flour. Lightly coat the bowl with oil.

4. Punch the dough down and knead it for 1 minute on a lightly floured surface. Divide the dough in half and reserve one half in a covered bowl set in a draft-free but cooler place (about 60°F.). (The cooler temperature helps to retard the dough's rising until you are ready to use it.) Place the other half of the dough on a lightly floured surface and pat and shape it into a rectangle 7 by 12 inches. Using a knife or a pizza wheel, cut from it three strips, each 1 inch wide and 12 inches long. Working on a lightly floured surface with one strip of dough at a time, use the palms of your hands to roll it into a rope that measures 24 inches long. Cut it into thirds to make three 8-inch pieces. Center one end of one of the pieces on the top of the inverted, oiled bowl and let it drape down the side of the bowl to the cookie sheet. Moisten the dough on top and, in the same way, add a second strip; when it reaches the cookie sheet, it should be about 2 inches from the first strip, but this measurement can be adjusted when all nine strips have been attached. Add the third strip in the same spokelike fashion (see illus. A).

ILLUSTRATION A

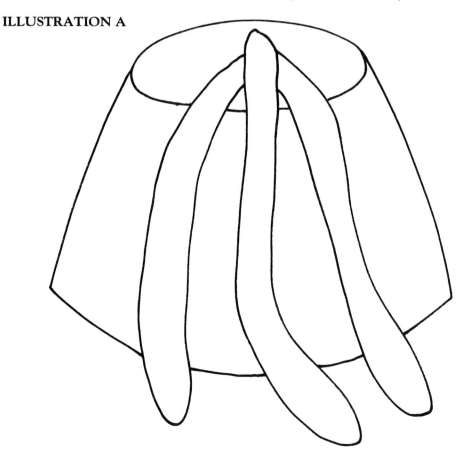

Then roll and cut into thirds the two remaining strips and add them in the same way around the bowl, moistening the top dough with water each time. Flatten the top (which will become the bottom of the basket when turned upright) with your hands so that the bread basket will sit flat when baked. Evenly space out the nine ropes of dough.

5. Cut the remaining piece of dough on your work surface into four strips, each 1 inch wide by 12 inches long. Working with one at a time, roll each to a length of 24 inches—these will be used to weave through the nine strips already on the bowl. Referring to illustration B, moisten the end of one of the ropes and pinch

ILLUSTRATION B

it in place under one of the lengths of dough already on the bowl, positioning it at the top of the bowl. Working toward the cookie sheet, begin weaving it through the nine strips, picking up one of the 8-inch lengths each time the weave is to go under it and moistening it with a bit of water to help hold it in place. When you reach the end of the rope, attach a second to it with a little water, hide the seam, and continue to weave. Depending on the size of your bowl, you may need all four ropes or only three. Gather any scraps, cover them, and set them aside. Using a sharp knife, trim the dough flush with the baking sheet all around. Cover the basket loosely with a linen towel or crumpled aluminum foil and let it rise until doubled in size, about 45 minutes. Meanwhile, preheat the oven to 375°F.

6. Make the braid: Since the bread basket will be baked upside down, a braid is added to cover the rough edge that will result. Combine any scraps of dough with the reserved dough and knead for 1 minute on a lightly floured surface. Pat or shape the dough into a rectangle 7 by 12 inches, about 1 inch thick, and cut from it three strips that are 1 inch wide and 12 inches long. Gather all the scraps, knead briefly, place them in a bowl, cover, and keep them in a cooler (60°F.), draft-free place until needed to make the rolls.

7. Working with one strip at a time on a lightly floured surface, roll each of the three lengths of dough into a rope that is 40 inches long. Occasionally lift the rope in the air or squeeze it to help elongate it. Cross the three ropes in the center and begin braiding from the center toward one end, ending 2 to 3 inches before reaching the ends. Then braid toward the other end, again stopping 2 to 3 inches short of the ends. Carefully pick up the braid and place it around the perimeter of the circle that you previously traced on one cookie sheet, positioning the inner edge of the braid on the line itself. To join the two ends, weave them into the braid design, attaching them by pinching them with a little water. Cover the braid and let rise in a warm (85°F.) place until doubled in bulk.

8. Glaze the basket: In a small bowl, place the remaining egg along with 1 teaspoon water; stir with a fork until smooth. When the basket has risen, uncover it and paint it with some of the egg glaze, making sure that it gets into each crevice. Bake the basket in the center of the preheated oven for 10 minutes, reduce the temperature to 350°F., and continue baking it for about 20 minutes, or until puffed and golden. Carefully remove the cookie sheet from the oven and slide the hot bowl onto your work surface. Using potholders, gently pick up the basket to remove it from the bowl, first sliding it around the bowl until it has loosened. Carefully place the bread basket, still inverted, directly on the oven rack and then bake it 10 minutes more, or until the inside of the bread is done but the outside is not too brown. Remove it from the oven, place it on a rack, and allow it to cool to room temperature. Increase the oven temperature to 375°F.

9. By this time, the braid should have risen to its maximum. Brush the braid with some of the egg glaze and bake it in the center of the oven for 10 minutes. Decrease the temperature to 350°F. and continue baking until the braid is done, about 20 minutes, or until the bread sounds hollow when the bottom is tapped; cool to room temperature. Increase the oven temperature to 375°F.

10. Meanwhile, shape the daisy rolls: Punch down all the remaining dough and knead it on a lightly floured surface for 1 minute. Pat or shape the dough on a lightly floured surface into a rectangle that measures 9 by 12 inches. Cut twelve strips, each ¾ inch wide and 12 inches long. Have ready, in separate bowls, the poppy seeds and the sunflower seeds. Also, have ready three lightly oiled, cool cookie sheets. Working with one strip at a time on a lightly floured surface, roll each strip into a rope that is 18 inches long. Cut each rope of dough into twelve 1½-inch lengths. Each daisy will require seven 1½-inch lengths of dough (six for petals and one for the center). Arrange the petals on the prepared cookie sheets, six flowers to a sheet, so that the petals are just touching in the center and the centers are open (see illus. C).

11. When one sheet is full, roll six of the 1½-inch lengths into balls. Coat one of them with the egg glaze and then dip one side into either the sunflower seeds or the poppy seeds. Repeat with the remaining balls, dipping all those with the sunflower-seed centers first, since the poppy seeds tend to stick in the egg glaze. Place each center, seed-side up, in the center of one of the daisies. Repeat with the remaining dough until you have 1½ dozen daisy rolls. Pat out any remaining

ILLUSTRATION C

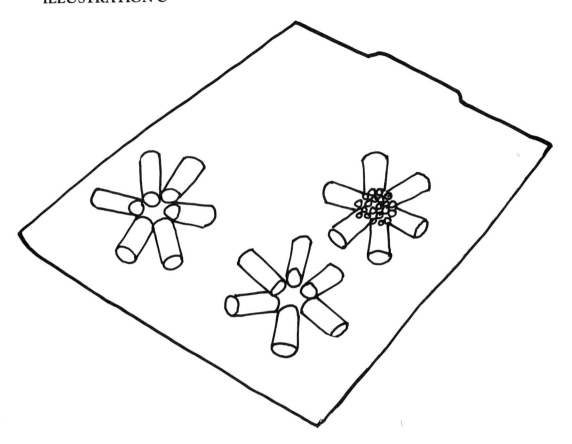

dough to a ¼-inch thickness, cut into leaf shapes, and intersperse them on the cookie sheets among the rolls. Loosely cover the sheets of rolls and leaves as they are completed and let rise until double in bulk. Uncover and brush the petals with more of the egg glaze. Then bake the leaves for about 5 minutes and the rolls for 12 to 15 minutes, or until done.

12. To arrange the bread basket: Turn the bread basket right side up and then top it with the braided ring, securing the ring to the basket with toothpicks. Fill the basket with the daisy rolls and leaves and serve the same day. The basket is completely edible too—just remove the toothpicks first.

Flavored Biscuits

Although I developed these highly flavored and decoratively shaped biscuits to be served with delicately prepared foods, such as a veal stew, simple omelette, or broiled seafood, I found that when made into smaller shapes, they are extremely popular as cocktail-party fare. You can even split them in two and make little sandwiches by filling them with sliced chicken or turkey, roast beef, ham, or shrimp salad.

As an accompaniment to an entrée, I often serve the Lemon-Parsley Biscuits, cut into fish shapes, with a seafood dinner, soup, or stew. The Chili-Corn Biscuits are so light and fluffy that I could make a meal of them alone, but they are also distinctive when served with roast pork or a glazed ham.

The Whole-Wheat Bacon Biscuits are complementary to roast chicken, veal roast, or oyster stew.

If you don't want to make the patterns, you can use deep, decorative cutters to shape the biscuits or simply cut them into squares or rounds. For cocktail-size biscuits, cut them with small cookie cutters, use a knife to cut them into sticks or 1-inch squares, or use a small glass to cut rounds.

How to Make Biscuit Patterns

Materials needed:
pen
tracing paper
scissors
lightweight cardboard

Trace the desired pattern on the tracing paper and cut it out with scissors. Place the cutout over the cardboard and trace around it. Cut out the cardboard shape to make the pattern.

Whole-Wheat Bacon Biscuits
MAKES 1 TO 1½ DOZEN, DEPENDING ON SHAPE,
OR ABOUT 5 DOZEN 1-INCH COCKTAIL-SIZE BISCUITS

½ pound lean, sliced, hickory-smoked bacon (about 12 slices)
1 medium-size onion, finely chopped (¾ cup)
¾ cup whole-wheat flour
¾ cup all-purpose flour
4 teaspoons baking powder
¼ teaspoon salt

¼ teaspoon freshly ground pepper
5 tablespoons chilled, unsalted butter, cut into thin slices
4 ounces sharp Cheddar cheese, coarsely shredded (1 cup)
½ cup sour cream, chilled
1 egg, lightly beaten

1. In a large, heavy skillet set over moderate heat, arrange the bacon in a single layer. Sauté, turning occasionally, until crisp and golden brown, about 15 minutes. (If the bacon is browning too quickly without the fat being rendered, reduce the heat slightly.) Remove from the skillet, reserving the fat, and drain on paper towels; crumble and reserve.

2. Pour off and discard all but 2 tablespoons of the fat. Let the fat in the skillet cool for 5 minutes. Add the onion and, over moderate heat, stirring frequently, sauté until it is softened, translucent, and lightly colored. Scrape up any brown bits clinging to the pan as you stir. Transfer the mixture to a small bowl and refrigerate until the drippings have chilled and solidified.

3. Preheat the oven to 425°F. Lightly oil a baking sheet. In a large mixing bowl, combine the whole-wheat flour, all-purpose flour, baking powder, salt, and pepper; stir to blend.

4. With a pastry blender or two knives, cut in the butter and chilled onion mixture until the mixture resembles coarse meal. Using a fork, quickly stir in the cheese, reserved bacon, and the sour cream.

5. Gather the dough into a ball (it will be soft) and, on a lightly floured surface, pat the dough out, turning it once so that both sides are coated with flour, to an 8-inch square about ¾ inch thick. Using one of the biscuit patterns and a sharp paring knife or a deep cookie cutter, cut out as many shapes as you can. As each is cut, carefully transfer it to the prepared baking sheet with a lightly floured spatula, leaving about 1 inch of space between biscuits. Gather the excess dough, wrap it tightly, and chill it until firm.

6. Meanwhile, use your fingers or a knife to smooth any ragged edges of the biscuits. Brush each biscuit with the beaten egg and set the sheet in the center of the oven. Bake the biscuits 12 to 14 minutes (about 10 minutes for 1-inch biscuits), or until they are puffed and golden brown. Transfer to a wire rack and cool for 3 to 5 minutes. Meanwhile, remove the excess dough from the refrigerator and repeat the procedure to make additional biscuits. As the biscuits are baked, wrap them in a linen napkin to keep them warm and place in a basket.

Chili-Corn Biscuits
MAKES 1 TO 1½ DOZEN, DEPENDING ON SHAPE, OR ABOUT
6 DOZEN 1-INCH COCKTAIL-SIZE BISCUITS

7 tablespoons chilled, unsalted
  butter, cut into thin slices
1 cup fresh corn kernels (from about
  2 ears of corn)
1 garlic clove, minced
1½ cups all-purpose flour
¼ cup yellow cornmeal
4 teaspoons baking powder
1 tablespoon sugar

½ teaspoon salt
½ cup sour cream, chilled
1 can (4 ounces) whole, roasted,
  peeled chilies, seeded, rinsed,
  drained, and chopped
6 ounces Monterey Jack or mild
  Cheddar cheese, coarsely shredded
  (1½ cups)
1 egg, lightly beaten

1. Lightly oil a baking sheet. Place 2 tablespoons of the butter in a small skillet over moderate heat along with the corn kernels and garlic; sauté, stirring frequently, for 3 to 5 minutes, depending on the tenderness of the corn, cooking the corn without browning the garlic. Transfer to a small plate and refrigerate until needed.

2. Preheat the oven to 425°F. In a large mixing bowl, combine the flour, cornmeal, baking powder, sugar, and salt. With a pastry blender or two knives, cut in the remaining butter until the mixture resembles coarse meal. Using a fork, quickly stir in the sour cream, chilies, cheese, and reserved corn-and-garlic mixture. Gather the dough into a soft ball and, on a lightly floured surface, pat the dough out, turning it once so that both sides are floured, to a 9-inch square about ¾ inch thick. Using one of the biscuit patterns and a sharp paring knife or small, deep cookie cutters, cut out as many shapes as you can. As each is cut, carefully transfer it with a lightly floured spatula to the prepared baking sheet, leaving about 1 inch of space between biscuits. Gather the excess dough, wrap it tightly, and chill it until firm.

3. Meanwhile, smooth any ragged edges of the biscuits with your fingers or trim them with a paring knife. Brush each with the beaten egg. Bake the biscuits in the center of the oven for 12 to 14 minutes (about 10 minutes for 1-inch biscuits), or until golden brown and baked through. Transfer to a wire rack and cool for 3 to 5 minutes before serving. Meanwhile, remove the excess dough from the refrigerator and repeat the procedure to make additional biscuits. As the biscuits are baked, wrap them in a linen napkin to keep them warm and place in a basket.

Lemon-Parsley Biscuits
MAKES 1 TO 1½ DOZEN, DEPENDING ON SHAPE, OR ABOUT
4 DOZEN 1-INCH COCKTAIL-SIZE BISCUITS

1½ cups all-purpose flour	rind (from 1 medium-size lemon)
4 teaspoons baking powder	¾ cup (loosely packed) finely
¼ teaspoon salt	chopped parsley
7 tablespoons chilled, unsalted	2 tablespoons fresh lemon juice
butter, cut into thin slices	½ cup plain yogurt
1 teaspoon (packed) grated lemon	1 egg, lightly beaten

1. Preheat the oven to 425°F. Lightly oil a baking sheet.

2. In a large mixing bowl, combine the flour, baking powder, and salt; stir to blend. With a pastry blender or two knives, cut in the butter until the mixture resembles coarse meal. Using a fork, stir in the lemon rind and parsley and then quickly stir in the lemon juice and yogurt. Stir just until the dough can be gathered into a soft ball.

3. On a lightly floured surface, pat the dough out, turning it once so that both sides are coated with flour, to a 7-inch square about ¾ inch thick. Using one of the biscuit patterns and a sharp paring knife or a deep cookie cutter, cut out as many shapes as you can. As each is cut, carefully transfer it to the prepared baking sheet with a lightly floured spatula, leaving about 1 inch of space between biscuits. Gather the excess dough, wrap it tightly, and chill it until firm.

4. Meanwhile, use your fingers to smooth any ragged edges of the biscuits or trim them with a knife. Brush each biscuit with the beaten egg. Bake the biscuits in the center of the oven for 12 to 14 minutes (about 10 minutes for 1-inch biscuits), or until they are puffed and golden brown. Transfer to a wire rack and cool for 3 to 5 minutes. Meanwhile, remove the excess dough from the refrigerator and repeat the procedure to make additional biscuits. As the biscuits are baked, wrap them in a linen napkin to keep them warm and place in a basket.

3
Fruits and Vegetables

Vegetable-Flower Arrangement with Three Dips

Y ou don't need a green thumb to create an elegant centerpiece of Carrot Chrysanthemums, Scallion Dahlias, Aster Leeks, Turnip Daisies, and American Beauty Radish Roses. In fact, all that you need to fashion raw vegetables into fabulous flowers is a sharp knife and some time on your hands.

Once you have made an assortment of these edible blossoms, they can be attached with toothpicks to celery stalks and arranged into a bouquet in a silver champagne bucket or wicker basket lined with a glass container (see instructions following). You can also use them to decorate a salad platter or a roast turkey. For an added touch, it is nice to garnish individual plates with a single crisp flower or two.

The flowers can be prepared hours ahead of time; in fact, some of the vegetables (carrots, leeks, and scallions) fluff up, "blossoming," after several hours in ice water to become even more spectacular. Serve the vegetables with any of the following dip recipes, which should be prepared a day ahead of time, and your guests will be truly feasting on flowers.

American Beauty Radish Roses
MAKES 10

10 *large radishes*   10 *small radishes*
10 *medium-size radishes*

1. Trim away and discard the root tip and stem end of each radish (see illus. A-1). Thinly slice (about $\frac{1}{16}$ inch thick) the small and medium-size radishes crosswise and shave each slice to a point so that it can be inserted into a large radish as a petal.

ILLUSTRATION A-1

2. Beginning near the stem end of each of the large radishes and working toward the root tip, make three rows of vertical downward cuts all around, turning the radish as you work and staggering the cuts (see illus. A-2). When you get to the root tip (now the top of the rose), make three cuts down ¼ inch into the flat surface where the root has been cut away. Insert a round toothpick into the stem end of each for adding to the flower bouquet later.

3. To make the petals for each flower, insert the beveled sides of slices from the medium and small radishes into each cut (see illus. A-3), using the largest slices at the bottom of the rose and working upward with progressively smaller slices. Place the roses in ice water for at least 1 hour.

ILLUSTRATION A-3

Carrot Chrysanthemums
MAKES 8

8 *large carrots, the larger the better*
1 *small carrot*

1. Using a swivel-bladed vegetable peeler, peel the carrots. Cut away enough of the stem end and root tip (see illus. B-1) to leave a 5-inch-long portion. Using a

ILLUSTRATION B-1

very sharp knife or vegetable slicer, cut the carrots lengthwise as thinly as possible, about $1/16$ inch thick; discard the rounded slices of carrot, reserving only the flat slices from the center. Cut the small carrot crosswise into slices $1/4$ inch thick.

2. Place one lengthwise slice on your work surface. Make two lengthwise cuts down the center of each slice, stopping about $3/4$ inch in from each end (see illus. B-2). Make two angled cuts at each side—begin the cuts about $3/4$ inch from each

ILLUSTRATION B-2

end and then run them off each side near the center (see illus. B-2 and B-3).

ILLUSTRATION B-3

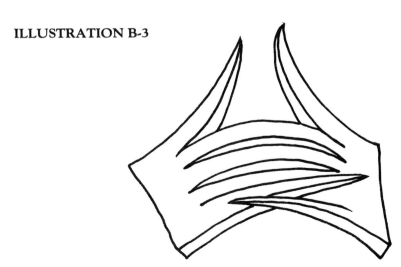

3. Bend one slice in half and secure the ends with a round toothpick (see illus. B-4). Repeat with two more slices, placing them directly over the preceding slice and securing them on the same toothpick. Insert the center of one of the small carrot slices over the toothpick tip in the center of the flower so that it will hold the "petals" in place. Keep in ice water for at least 1 hour.

4. Repeat steps 2 and 3 with the remaining carrot strips to make more flowers and keep in ice water for 1 hour.

Turnip Daisies
MAKES 12

    3 *medium-size white turnips*
    1 *small carrot*

1. Using a swivel-bladed vegetable peeler, peel the turnips and the carrot. Cut away and discard the root and stem end of the turnips (see illus. C-1). Slice the

ILLUSTRATION C-1

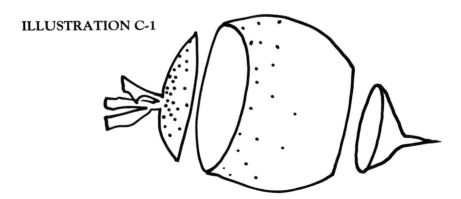

turnips and the carrot crosswise about ¼ inch thick; reserve the carrot slices in cold water.

2. Working with one turnip slice, cut seven petals by removing the area between petals but leaving about ½ to ¾ inch uncut turnip in the center (see illus. C-2).

ILLUSTRATION C-2

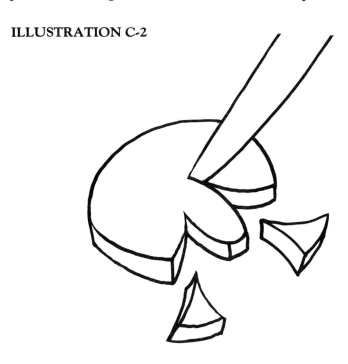

Note that each shape you cut away is of the same size—if you cut one successfully, it will be easier to cut all of them. Also note that the tip of each petal is left uncut so that the end of each is flat.

3. As you complete each daisy, push it onto a toothpick so that the tip of the pick extends ⅛ inch through the center of the daisy; push a carrot slice over the extended pick to create the center of the daisy (see illus. C-3). Place in ice water until ready to arrange.

ILLUSTRATION C-3

Scallion Dahlias and Aster Leeks

The technique for making both types of flowers here is exactly the same—the Scallion Dahlia is simply a smaller version of the Aster Leek—so they have been combined in the following instructions.

MAKES 14

6 *medium-size leeks*
8 *large scallions*

1. Cut away and discard enough of the root end and green portions of the leeks and scallions to leave 2-inch lengths of scallion and 3-inch lengths of leek (see illus. D-1). Push a round toothpick ¾ inch into the root end of each (see illus. D-2).

ILLUSTRATION D-1

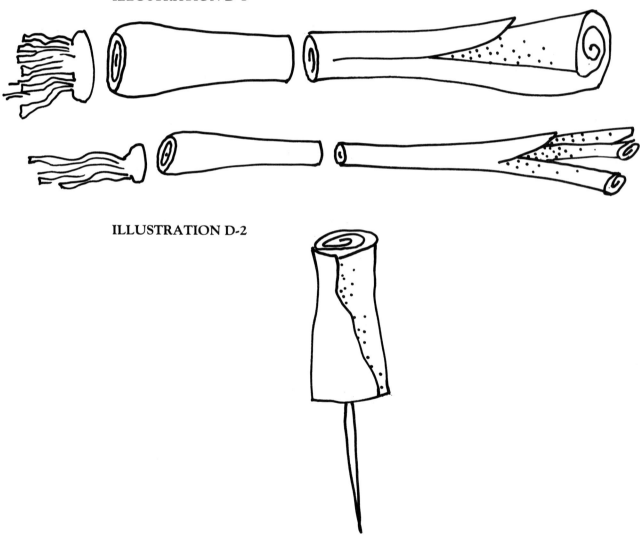

ILLUSTRATION D-2

2. Working one at a time, place a leek or scallion on a cutting board. Beginning ½ to ¾ inch from the root end, make parallel cuts, ⅛ inch apart, through the center of the leek or scallion (see illus. D-3). Gently spread the petals outward

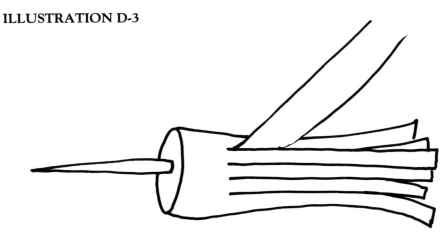

with your fingers and place the vegetables in ice water for at least 1 hour, occasionally spreading the petals outward to fluff them up. The petals will spread and curl outward as they are chilled in the ice water (see illus. D-4).

ILLUSTRATION D-4

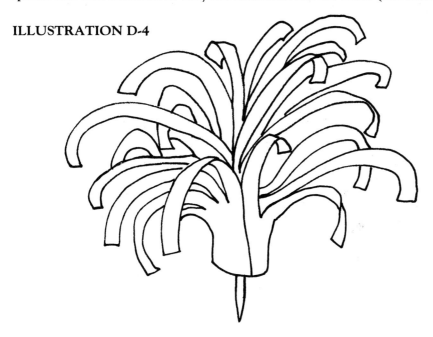

Arranging the Bouquet

Choose a ceramic or glass vase or bowl, a silver champagne bucket, a wicker basket, or even a red clay flowerpot for your arrangement. If you are using a vessel that won't hold water, line it with a bowl or vase and, if you wish, set a metal florist's frog or flower holder in the bottom. Fill the container with ice water. Place the tallest celery rib in the center, adding progressively shorter ribs to the arrangement as the sides of the container are reached. Then attach any variety or combination of flowers to the celery by pushing the toothpicks inserted in them into the tops and sides of the celery ribs. For greenery, insert parsley or lettuce leaves and green beans attached to wooden shish-kebab skewers or toothpicks between the flowers. To keep the arrangement fresh, lightly spray it with cold water once in a while until serving time. If you'd rather not disturb your arrangement, cut additional vegetable flowers to serve with the assortment of dips.

Blue-Cheese-Walnut Dip
MAKES ABOUT 2½ CUPS

1 *pint sour cream*
½ *cup packed blue cheese, crumbled*

¼ *cup finely chopped walnuts*
freshly ground pepper to taste

1. In a medium-size bowl, place the sour cream and beat it with a spoon until smooth. Add the blue cheese and stir until blended.

2. Reserve 1 tablespoon of the walnuts for garnish; stir in the remaining walnuts along with pepper to taste. Cover and refrigerate overnight.

3. Vigorously stir the dip and transfer it to a serving dish. Garnish with the remaining chopped walnuts.

Bacon-Horseradish Dip
MAKES ABOUT 2 CUPS

1 *pint sour cream*
8 *slices bacon, crisp-cooked and drained*

1 *to 2 tablespoons prepared horseradish, drained*
salt and freshly ground pepper to taste

1. In a medium-size mixing bowl, place the sour cream and beat it with a spoon until smooth.

2. Crumble seven slices of the bacon and stir them into the sour cream along with 1 tablespoon of the horseradish. Taste for seasoning; if you want a hotter dip, add the remaining horseradish. Add the salt and pepper to taste. Cover tightly and refrigerate overnight. Crumble the remaining slice of bacon, wrap, and store in the refrigerator.

3. To serve, stir the dip and then transfer it to a serving dish. Sprinkle the reserved crumbled bacon over the top.

Lemon-Dill Dip
MAKES ABOUT 2 CUPS

1 *pint sour cream*
2 *tablespoons snipped fresh dill or*
1 *tablespoon dried, crumbled*
2 *to 3 tablespoons fresh lemon juice*

salt and freshly ground pepper to taste
Garnish:
sprig of dill or parsley

1. In a medium-size bowl, place the sour cream and beat it with a spoon until smooth.

2. Stir in the dill and 2 tablespoons of the lemon juice. Taste for seasoning; if you want a more tart dip, add the remaining lemon juice. Stir in the salt and pepper to taste. Cover and refrigerate overnight.

3. To serve, vigorously stir the dip, transfer it to a serving dish, and garnish with the sprig of dill or parsley.

Carved Fruits

(Photographs on pages 3 and 95)

When artfully carved, fruit will provide a rainbow of color to a buffet table. You may want to recreate all the following designs and arrange them into a centerpiece for a party, or you can simply choose one and serve it at a breakfast or luncheon. If you like to serve fresh fruit for dessert, a splendid array of carved fruit can be just as dramatic as an elegant dessert that took all day to prepare—and it will contain a fraction of the calories.

With a few simple cutting techniques, you can easily make any of the designs shown. Be sure to start with firm, ripe fruit without blemishes.

Quartered Pineapple Wedges

Using a sharp chef's knife, cut away and discard about 1 inch from the bottom of the pineapple. Keeping the leafy green stem intact, cut the pineapple and stem lengthwise in quarters (illus. A-1).

ILLUSTRATION A-1

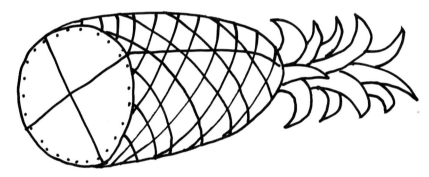

Using a sharp paring knife, cut the flesh away from the skin, leaving a ½-inch-thick shell (see illus. A-2). Remove the cut portion from the shell. Slice

ILLUSTRATION A-2

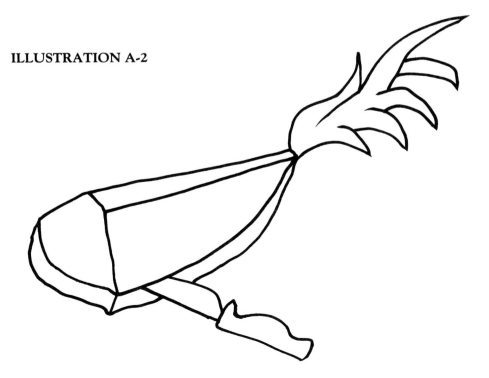

away and discard the core. Cut the pineapple flesh into wedges about ½ inch thick (see illus. A-3). Return the wedges to the shell, offsetting every other one to create a pattern (see illus. A-4).

ILLUSTRATION A-3

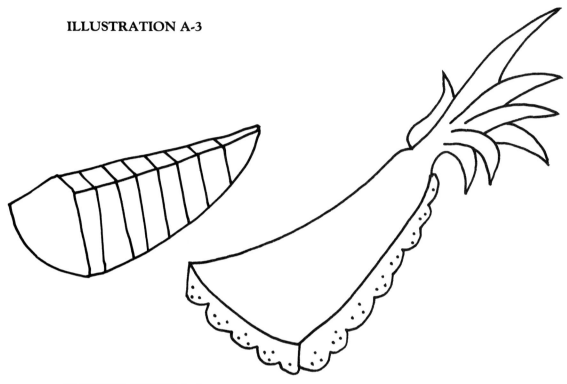

ILLUSTRATION A-4

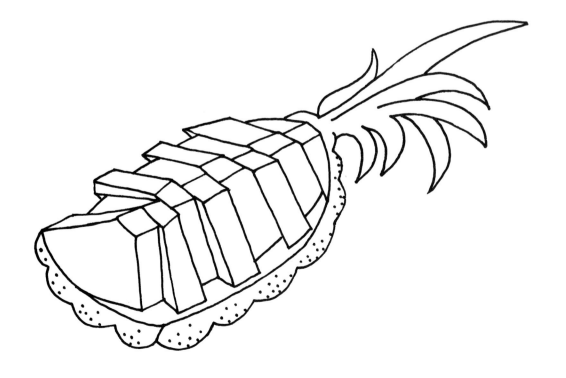

Zigzag Melons and Papayas

Using a sharp chef's knife, cut away about 2 inches from the blunt end of a papaya or from either end of a melon (see illus. B-1). Reserve the cut portion for another use, such as a fruit salad.

ILLUSTRATION B-1

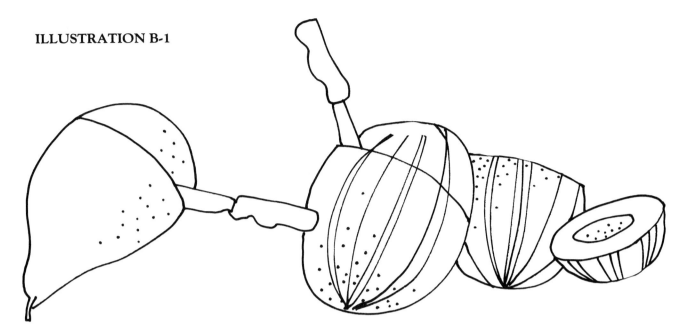

With the cut side of the papaya or melon upward on your work surface, cut triangles 3 to 4 inches long and 1½ to 2 inches wide, depending on the size of the fruit, all around the fruit (see ills. B-2). Try to make the triangles as even as

ILLUSTRATION B-2

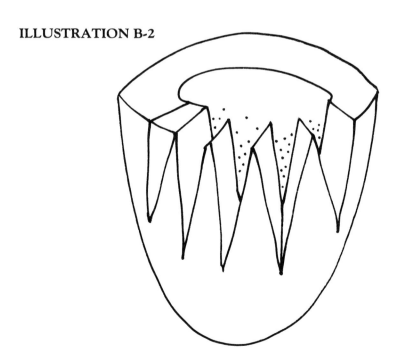

possible. Reserve the cutout triangles for another use. Scoop out the seeds remaining in the shell with a spoon.

Orange and Grapefruit Cubes

Using a sharp chef's knife, cut away about ½ inch from the top of an orange or grapefruit (see illus. C-1). Cut downward about ½ inch from each of two

ILLUSTRATION C-1

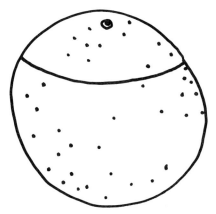

opposing sides almost to the base of the fruit (see illus. C-2). Cut the remaining two sides almost down to the base as you did with the previous two sides (see

ILLUSTRATION C-2

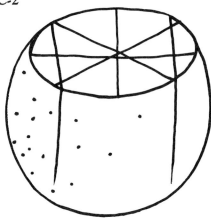

illus. C-3). Carefully pull the four cut sides about ½ inch out from the inner cube (illus. C-4).

ILLUSTRATION C-3

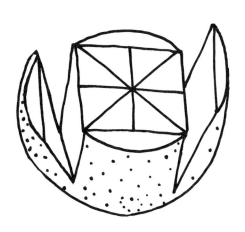

ILLUSTRATION C-4

Spiral Pineapple

Using the leafy green top of the pineapple as a handle and a sharp chef's knife, remove the skin of the pineapple but leave the "eyes" in the fruit's flesh (see illus. D-1). Holding a sharp knife at a 45-degree angle to the pineapple and

ILLUSTRATION D-1

working from the top of the pineapple to the bottom, cut along one side of one row of eyes; when the cut reaches the bottom of the pineapple, remove the knife and return to the top of the pineapple. Make a second cut parallel to the first but at an opposite 45-degree angle (see illus. D-2) in order to remove the entire spiral of eyes and create a groove in its place. Continue until all the spirals of eyes have been removed, using the leafy green top as a "handle" as before.

ILLUSTRATION D-2

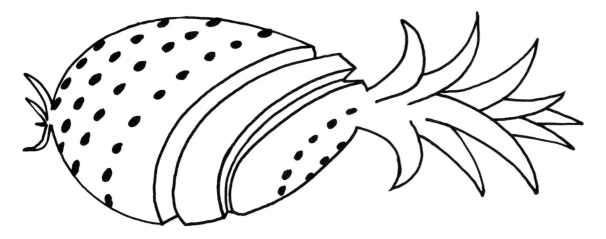

Watermelon Wedges

Cut a large, ripe watermelon lengthwise into thin wedges. Arrange the wedges in a spoke design on a large flat wicker tray or basket. Place a grapefruit or melon in the center.

Vegetarian Sushi

(Photograph on page 6)

It is unfortunate that so many people associate sushi only with raw fish because the Japanese make many exotic yet delicious varieties of vegetarian sushi. Although vegetarian sushi is frequently eaten along with sushi made of raw seafood, only vegetarian sushi recipes have been included here, partly because most of us don't live close enough to the ocean or a first-rate sushi bar to get really fresh fish.

Today in Japan, many innovative chefs have ventured into new ways of making sushi. Although I have included here a recipe for classic fishless sushi of cucumber and sesame seed *(kappa-maki)*, I, too, have been creative with the remaining two recipes. For instance, the technique used for making Mushroom Sushi is the same as it has been for hundreds of years—that is, the preparation begins with Sushi Rice and *nori* seaweed—but, to compose the central core, I have combined ingredients only close to traditional. The third recipe—Cabbage-Wrapped Sushi—is a very distant cousin to any classic sushi. It contains neither rice nor seaweed, but, instead, it begins with a leaf of green cabbage rolled around spinach, carrots, and turnips. Because the cabbage wrapper will retain its moisture content much longer than the usual seaweed wrapper, it can be prepared up to six hours ahead of time.

To serve sushi Japanese-style, place a mound of prepared *wasabi* (about ½ teaspoon) at the edge of small, individual, square Japanese dishes and add about 1 tablespoon of soy sauce to each. The diner can then mix the two together and use it as a dipping sauce for the sushi, or he can touch the *wasabi* with the sushi (preferably held with chopsticks) and then dip it into the soy sauce. Finally, arrange about 1 teaspoon of pink or red pickled ginger slices on individual sushi plates to be eaten between bites of sushi as a flavor complement.

For an explanation of special Japanese ingredients required for these recipes, see below. You will also need a bamboo rolling mat to form the rolls for the Mushroom Sushi and the Cucumber-and-Sesame-Seed Sushi.

Special Ingredients and Information

Sushi is very enjoyable and rewarding to make. True, there are some special ingredients that you might have to send for if you don't live near an Oriental market that carries them, but the ingredients will all keep well for many months and there really are no satisfactory substitutes.

Since there are hundreds of mail-order firms that sell these special ingredients, the easiest way to find the nearest source is to write the Japanese Food Corporation, 445 Kaufman Court, South San Francisco, California

94080; they are one of the largest suppliers and importers of Oriental foods in the United States.

- **Wasabi:** This is a special and very hot green horseradish. You can buy it in powder form (the smallest can is 1 ounce but, because it is so hot, it should last a long time) or already prepared in a tube. To prepare 2 tablespoons of *wasabi* from powder, simply put 2 level tablespoons in a small bowl and stir in 4 to 5 teaspoons of water to make a paste; let it rest, covered, for 10 minutes or up to 8 hours before using.

- **Nori:** Made of seaweed that is pressed into thin, paperlike sheets, *nori* is used to wrap most rolls of sushi. Since it should remain dry, it is best to eat sushi as soon as possible after preparing. It usually comes in packages of seven sheets (each about 7½ by 8 inches), which are then cut in half. It must be stored in a dry place.

- **Rice vinegar:** Made from rice, this vinegar is of a very high quality. When mixed with a little sugar, it adds a subtle flavor to sushi rice.

- **Rice:** Rice used for sushi should be the traditional short-grain rice often labeled Blue Rose or California Rose.

- **Japanese soy sauce (*shoyu*):** This has a lighter flavor than Chinese soy sauce and a distinctively different flavor. Kikkoman is the most common brand available in the United States.

- **Pink or red pickled ginger:** Although you can make this at home with fresh gingerroot, only the sprouts that appear for a short time during the spring work. Consequently, it is better to buy it. Since it comes in vacuum-sealed pouches, you can send for it through the mail if you cannot find it locally. Refrigerate unused pickled ginger, along with any brine, in a jar with a tightly fitted lid. It will keep for many months because it has been pickled.

- **Bamboo sushi-rolling mat (*makisu*):** This indispensable utensil for rolling sushi is made of slender round strips of bamboo tied together with string.

Sushi Rice

Properly made, sushi rice should be flavorful and sticky enough to hold together when the sushi is formed. To achieve the desired results, you must begin with Japanese short-grain rice and rice vinegar. Cooked sushi rice is used at room temperature, but it can be made as long as 8 hours ahead of time and kept covered with a damp cloth until needed.

MAKES ABOUT 3 CUPS

1 cup plus 2 level tablespoons Japanese short-grain rice	2 tablespoons sugar
2 tablespoons rice vinegar	1 teaspoon salt

1. Line a colander with a double layer of cheesecloth that is large enough to extend over the edges, add the rice, and rinse under cold running water for about 3 minutes. Then, set the colander of rice in a bowl or pan and run cold water into it until the rice is covered; let it rest for 10 minutes and drain. Repeat this rinsing and soaking procedure three times, or until the rinsing water is clear, reducing the rinsing time to 30 seconds instead of 3 minutes. Gather the cheesecloth into a pouch around the rice and squeeze to remove as much of the water as possible.

2. In a small, noncorrosive saucepan, combine the vinegar, sugar, and salt; place over low heat and, stirring occasionally, heat until the sugar and salt have dissolved. Remove from the heat and set aside to cool to room temperature.

3. Place the rice in a heavy, medium-size pot that has a tight-fitting lid. Add 1⅓ cups cold water and place the pan over high heat. Bring the water to a full boil, stirring only once as it begins to boil. Reduce the heat to moderate, tightly cover the pot, preferably weighting the lid with a heavy object such as a brick, and boil for 5 minutes. Without lifting the lid, reduce the heat as low as possible and still maintain a simmer, and cook until all the water has been absorbed, 12 to 15 minutes, checking only once or twice during the final 5 minutes of cooking to prevent steam from escaping. Remove the pan from the heat, remove the lid, place two layers of paper towels over the pan, and return the lid. Let the rice rest for 10 minutes. (This resting period completes the cooking of the rice while the paper towels prevent the moisture that collects on the underside of the lid from dripping back onto the rice.) Remove the lid and paper towels.

4. Evenly spread the rice over a medium-size (about 8 by 10 inches), shallow, glass or ceramic dish or noncorrosive baking pan. Slowly drizzle half the vinegar mixture over the rice, using a piece of cardboard to fan it as you pour. This cools the rice (in Japan, a special fan is used). Using a fork, rake the grains back and forth into rows, both lengthwise and crosswise, to separate the grains and hasten the cooling. Add the remaining vinegar mixture and continue to fan and separate the grains until they have cooled. Run cold water over several layers of paper towels or a kitchen towel, wring out gently, and place over the rice until serving time, up to 8 hours before. Use with either of the following sushi recipes.

Cucumber and Sesame-Seed Sushi

Strips of crisp cucumber sprinkled with toasted sesame seeds make up the core of this sushi variety. A wrapping of nori *and the addition of Sushi Rice complete this delicious, traditional vegetarian sushi, known as* kappa-maki *in Japan.*

MAKES 6 ROLLS (two servings if served alone or six servings if served with two other varieties of sushi)

2 kirby cucumbers, each about 4 inches long (3 to 4 ounces each)

2 tablespoons sesame seeds

3 sheets (about 7½ by 8 inches each) nori, each cut in half crosswise with scissors or a sharp knife

3 cups prepared Sushi Rice (recipe precedes)

1½ teaspoons prepared wasabi (see p. 73)

Accompaniments:
   prepared wasabi (see p. 73)
   Japanese soy sauce
   pink or red pickled ginger

1. Prepare the cucumbers: Peel the cucumbers and trim the ends. Cut them in half lengthwise and, using a spoon, scoop out and discard the seeds. Cut the cucumbers lengthwise into strips ¼ inch wide. Cover and set aside for up to 1 hour before assembling the sushi.

2. Toast the sesame seeds: Place the sesame seeds in a small skillet or saucepan over moderate heat and, stirring constantly, cook until they turn golden brown and begin to pop. Remove from the heat and set aside until needed.

3. Assemble the sushi: Place one sheet of *nori* shiny side down on top of the bamboo sushi-rolling mat with one end extending ½ inch beyond the edge closest to you (see illus. A-1). Dip your hands in cold water and shake off the

ILLUSTRATION A-1

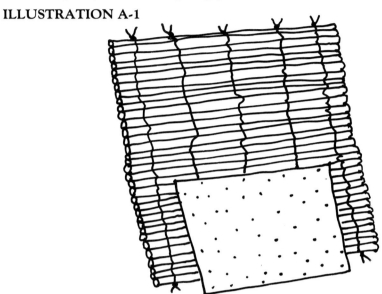

excess. Spread ½ cup of the Sushi Rice evenly over the *nori*, leaving uncovered ½ inch at the top (the edge farthest from you) and ¼ inch at each of the other three edges (see illus. A-2). Using one damp finger, make a slight horizontal indention

ILLUSTRATION A-2

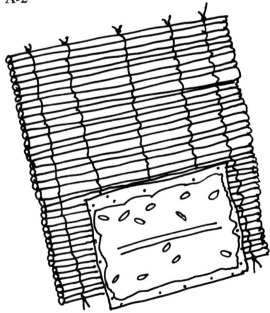

across the center of the rice (see illus. A-2). Spread the indention evenly with about ¼ teaspoon of the *wasabi*. Arrange two rows of cucumber strips across the top of the *wasabi*, trimming them to fit if necessary. Sprinkle the cucumber strips with 1 teaspoon of the toasted sesame seeds.

4. Holding the core of ingredients in the center with your fingertips and beginning with the edge nearest you, tightly roll the sushi in the mat (see illus.

ILLUSTRATION A-3

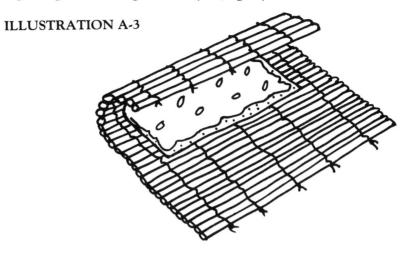

A-3). Then firmly press the roll into a square shape (see illus. A-4). Unroll the

ILLUSTRATION A-4

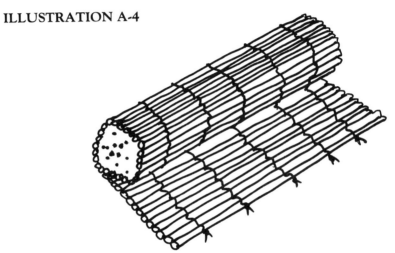

mat, pick up the sushi roll and place it on a cutting board. Make two more rolls using the remaining ingredients and then place them on the cutting board along with the first one.

5. Cut the sushi rolls: Using a very sharp knife, cut one roll crosswise through the center (see illus. B-1). Place the two halves next to each other (see illus. B-2) and cut them at the same time into three equal, crosswise pieces. Repeat with the remaining five rolls. Place the pieces upright on a plate in groups of six (see illus. B-3) and serve with the accompaniments.

ILLUSTRATION B-1   ILLUSTRATION B-2   ILLUSTRATION B-3

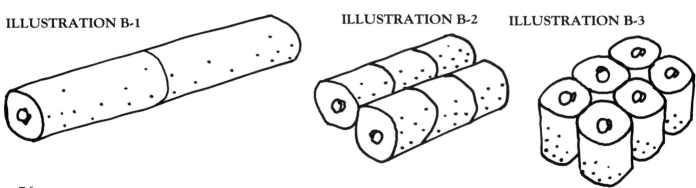

Mushroom Sushi

Japanese dried mushrooms (shiitake), sometimes referred to as "imported forest mushrooms," give this sushi a "meaty" taste. A central core of marinated shiitake, strips of egg, wasabi, and red bell pepper are encased in Sushi Rice and nori.

MAKES 6 ROLLS (two servings if served alone or six servings if served with two other varieties of sushi)

Mushrooms:
  6 *medium-size (½ ounce) dried shiitake or imported forest mushrooms*
  2 *cups boiling water*
  1 *tablespoon Oriental sesame oil*
  1 *tablespoon Japanese soy sauce*

Pepper:
  1 *medium-size red bell pepper (or green if red is not available)*

Egg Center:
  1 *egg*
  2 *teaspoons sugar*
  ¼ *teaspoon salt*
  1 *teaspoon all-purpose flour*

  1 *teaspoon vegetable oil*

Assembly:
  3 *sheets (about 7½ by 8 inches each) nori, each cut in half crosswise with scissors or a sharp knife*

Rice:
  3 *cups prepared Sushi Rice (recipe precedes)*
  1½ *teaspoons prepared wasabi (see p. 73)*

Accompaniments:
  prepared wasabi (see p. 73)
  Japanese soy sauce
  red or pink pickled ginger

1. Prepare the mushrooms: Place the *shiitake* in a medium-size, heatproof bowl and pour the boiling water over them. Let them rest for 30 minutes, stirring occasionally. Drain the mushrooms (reserve the liquid, if desired, for another use, such as an addition to soup) and squeeze as much liquid from them as possible. Cut off and discard the tough stems. Slice the mushroom caps into strips slightly wider than ⅛ inch. Place the strips in a small bowl and stir in the sesame oil and soy sauce; let them marinate, stirring occasionally, for at least 1 hour or as long as 8 hours (cover if preparing ahead of time). Set aside at room temperature until needed.

2. Prepare the bell pepper: Cut off the top and bottom of the pepper and discard. Cut the pepper in half lengthwise and discard the seeds and ribs. Cut one half lengthwise into strips ¼ inch wide; reserve the other half in case it is needed for more strips at the time of assembly. The pepper strips may be kept, covered, at room temperature for several hours before using.

3. Prepare the egg center: In a medium-size bowl, whisk or stir together the egg, sugar, salt, and flour until smooth. Place the oil in a small (6- or 7-inch), heavy skillet set over moderate heat. When the oil is hot, pour in the egg mixture and immediately reduce the heat to low. Cover the pan and cook it gently until the top has set, about 3 minutes. After 1½ minutes, lift the edge of the egg with the tines of a fork to make sure that the bottom of the egg is not browning; if it is, reduce the heat further. When done, the top should be just set. Transfer the egg to a paper towel and cover it with plastic wrap. When the egg is cool, cut away and discard about ¼ inch all around the edge. Cut the remaining round of egg into strips ¼ inch wide. Cover and set aside for up to 2 hours.

4. Assemble the sushi: Place one sheet of *nori* shiny side down on top of the bamboo sushi-rolling mat with one end extending ½ inch beyond the edge closest to you (see illus. A-1). Dip your hands in cold water and shake off the excess. Spread ½ cup of the Sushi Rice evenly over the *nori*, leaving uncovered ½ inch at the top (the edge farthest from you) and ¼ inch at each of the other three edges (see illus. A-2). Using one damp finger, make a slight horizontal indention across the center of the rice (see illus. A-2). Spread the indention evenly with about ¼ teaspoon of the *wasabi*. Arrange one-sixth of the marinated mushroom strips over the *wasabi* and then arrange a row (about three strips) of red pepper across the center, trimming the strips to fit if necessary. On each side of the red-pepper row, add a row of egg strips, overlapping them if necessary to fit.

5. Holding the core of ingredients in the center with your fingertips and beginning with the edge nearest you, tightly roll the sushi in the mat (see illus. A-3). Then firmly press the roll into a square shape (see illus. A-4). Unroll the mat, pick up the sushi roll, place it on a cutting board. Make two additional rolls with the remaining ingredients and then place them on the cutting board along with the first one.

6. Cut the sushi rolls: Using a very sharp knife, cut one roll crosswise through the center (see illus. B-1). Place the two halves next to each other (see illus. B-2) and cut them at the same time into three equal, crosswise pieces. Repeat with the remaining five rolls. Place the pieces upright on a plate in groups of six (see illus. B-3) and serve with the accompaniments.

Cabbage-Wrapped Sushi

Here is an innovative sushi that does not require the use of a bamboo-rolling mat, Sushi Rice, or nori. It also has an advantage that other varieties of sushi do not have—the rolls can be prepared and, covered, held at room temperature for about four hours before serving. Chopped spinach replaces the rice used to make traditional sushi, while shredded, marinated carrots and turnip sticks make up the central core of the roll. Besides being attractive to look at, Cabbage-Wrapped Sushi is a tasty addition to the vegetarian sushi assortment.

MAKES 6 ROLLS (two servings if served alone or six servings if served with two other varieties of sushi)

1½ pounds fresh spinach with stems
  ¼ teaspoon salt
  6 large (8 inches each) green
    cabbage leaves (see Note)
  1 medium-size (about 6 ounces)
    white turnip
  1 tablespoon vegetable oil
  4 medium-size (8 ounces) carrots,

    peeled and coarsely shredded (1½
    cups packed)
  1 tablespoon Japanese soy sauce
  1 tablespoon Oriental sesame oil

Accompaniments:
  prepared wasabi (see p. 73)
  Japanese soy sauce
  pink or red pickled ginger

Note: To remove the cabbage leaves, use a sharp knife to cut out the core (3 to 4 inches in diameter); the leaves will then easily peel off.

1. Soak the spinach in a large bowl or sinkful of cold water, shaking it occasionally to help dislodge any sand that may be clinging to the leaves. Drain well, rinse, and drain again. Remove the stems and discard them. In a large, heavy pot, place the spinach, with only the water that clings to the leaves, and set over moderately high heat; cover and cook only until the bulk has reduced and the leaves are wilted, 3 to 4 minutes. Drain in a colander set over a bowl, pushing on the spinach with the back of a spoon to extract as much liquid as possible (reserve it for a soup). Chop the spinach (you should have about 1½ cups) and set aside for up to 1 hour.

2. Fill a large, heavy pot with water, add the salt, cover, and bring the water to a boil over high heat. Add the cabbage leaves, and when the boiling resumes, boil, covered, for about 5 minutes, or until the leaves are just tender. Remove the leaves with a slotted spoon and reserve the water. Drain the leaves, cover them, and cool to room temperature. The leaves can be prepared as long as an hour before the sushi is assembled.

3. Return the water in which the cabbage was cooked to a boil. Meanwhile, trim the ends from the turnip and peel it with a vegetable peeler. Cut it into ⅜-inch julienne, using the width of the turnip as the length of the julienne. Drop them into the boiling water and, when the boiling resumes, cook for 3 to 4 minutes, or until just tender but slightly resistant to the bite. Rinse under cold running water; pat dry, cover, and set aside until ready to assemble the sushi. The turnips can be prepared as long as an hour before the sushi is assembled.

4. Place the vegetable oil in a heavy, medium-size skillet (preferably nonstick) over moderately high heat. When the oil is hot but not smoking, add the carrot shreds and cook, stirring frequently, until they begin to caramelize and turn slightly brown, 4 to 5 minutes; if they brown too quickly, reduce the heat to moderate and continue cooking. The carrots should still be firm to the bite when done and should measure about ¾ cup. Transfer them to a small, heatproof bowl and stir in the soy sauce and sesame oil. Let cool to room temperature and then cover until needed. The carrots can be prepared at least as long as an hour before the sushi is assembled.

5. Assemble the sushi: Using a knife, cut away and discard the raised portion of the vein of each cabbage leaf. Place one leaf, deveined side down, on your work surface. Arrange about ¼ cup of the chopped spinach across the lower third of the leaf, making a slight indention across the center. Arrange one-sixth of the carrot shreds over the indention and top it with a row of turnip sticks (about three), trimming them to fit if necessary. Fold the stem end of the cabbage leaf over the filling and then tightly roll it to enclose the filling. Place the sushi roll on a plate, seam side down, and continue making rolls with the remaining ingredients. Trim off and discard about ½ inch from each end to make them even. Cover and keep at room temperature until ready to serve, up to 4 hours ahead of time.

6. Cut the sushi rolls: Using a sharp knife, cut one roll in half crosswise (see illus. B-1). Place the two halves next to each other (see illus. B-2) and cut them at the same time into three equal lengths to make six rounds of sushi. Repeat with the remaining five rolls. Place the pieces upright on a plate in groups of six (see illus. B-3) and serve with the accompaniments.

Strawberry Shortbread Baskets

Remember when you could buy strawberries piled high in old-fashioned wooden berry baskets instead of the green plastic ones around today? With a few exceptions, such as at roadside stands in the country, those days are pretty much past. This is unfortunate because not only did the wooden boxes seem to hold more berries, but they were more ecological too, because regular customers returned their empty baskets to be refilled.

Now, you can make your own old-fashioned berry basket for your strawberries, and eat it too. First you dip the berries into a shiny glaze and then you mound them in an edible basket of shortbread until they almost topple over. Serve the berry baskets with whipped cream for a luscious change-of-pace dessert.

Strawberry Shortbread Baskets

Plan to chill the shortbread dough for this recipe for at least two hours or as long as overnight.

8 SERVINGS (makes two baskets)

Cream-Cheese Shortbread:
1 *package (8 ounces) cream cheese, at room temperature*
1 *cup (2 sticks) unsalted butter, at room temperature*
¾ *cup plus 4 tablespoons sugar*
3½ *cups all-purpose flour*

Assembly:
1 *egg white*
pinch of salt
1 *cup sifted confectioner's sugar*
3 *pints strawberries*
1 *jar (10 ounces) apple jelly*
½ *pint heavy cream, whipped*

1. Prepare the dough: In a large mixing bowl, beat the cream cheese and butter together until smooth. Add the ¾ cup sugar and beat until fluffy. Stir in about half the flour and mix until smooth. Blend in the remaining flour to make a stiff dough. Divide the dough in half and shape each into a flat round. Wrap each separately and refrigerate for at least 2 hours or as long as overnight. Meanwhile, make two paper patterns, one that is a 4-inch square, and the other, a strip that measures ⅝ inch wide by 5½ inches long.

2. Make the cookies: Preheat the oven to 350°F. On a lightly floured surface with a floured rolling pin, roll out half the dough until it is ¼ inch thick. Using a paring knife and the square pattern, cut out five squares; using the ⅝- by 5½-inch pattern, cut out four strips. With a floured spatula, transfer the shapes to an ungreased baking sheet, leaving 1 inch between them. Also transfer as many of the excess pieces of dough as will fit on the baking sheet without crowding to make the cookie crumbs needed in the final assembly. Sprinkle 2 tablespoons of the remaining granulated sugar evenly over the squares and strips. Bake for about 15 minutes, or until the strips and small pieces are light golden brown and firm. Remove the sheet from the oven and carefully transfer the strips and small pieces to a rack to cool. Return the squares to the oven and bake until they, too, are light golden brown and firm. Transfer to racks and cool. Repeat with the remaining dough to make the pieces for the second basket. When cool, finely grind or crush enough of the excess pieces to make ½ cup; set aside.

3. Construct the strawberry baskets: In a medium-size bowl, whisk or beat the egg white with the pinch of salt until frothy. Add half the confectioner's sugar and continue to beat. Add the remaining confectioner's sugar and beat until smooth. Stir in the reserved cookie crumbs to make a sticky frosting. The mixture should be moist enough to "glue" two cookies together; if it is too dry, add a few drops of water. Cover the bowl until needed.

4. Reserve two of the cookie squares for the bottoms of the two baskets. To make the sides of each basket, place four of the cookie squares, sugared sides up, on your work surface. Using a butter knife, spread a line of frosting about ¼ inch wide and ⅛ inch thick along the top of one edge of each of the four squares (see illus. A). Press one of the four strips of cookie into the frosting on each

ILLUSTRATION A

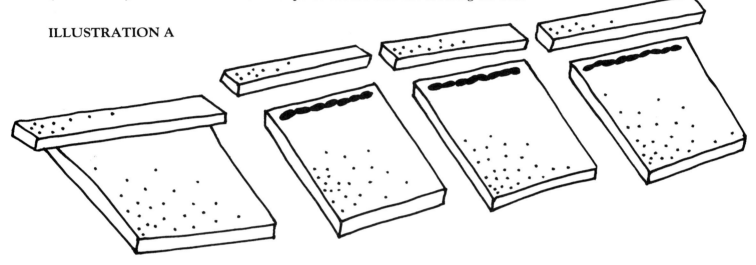

square, making sure that each is centered and that the outer edge is flush with the edge of each square. Repeat with the remaining four squares and four strips to make the pieces for the second basket. Let the frosting dry until hard, about 3 hours.

5. When the frosting has dried, place a sheet of waxed paper on your work surface and center one of the remaining cookie squares, sugared side up, on it. Gather eight heavy cans or jars to use to support the sides of the basket as you "glue" them together with frosting. (If the frosting has become firm, stir in a few drops of water.) Referring to illustration B, apply a line of frosting about ⅛ inch

ILLUSTRATION B

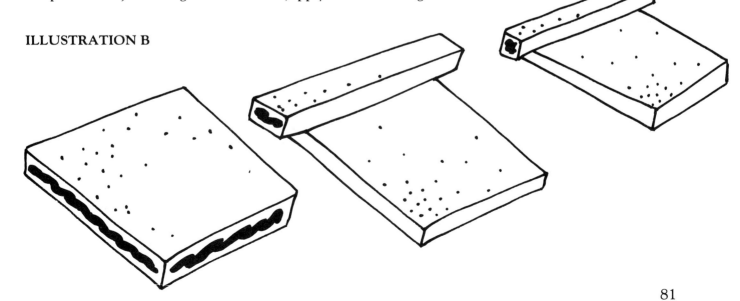

thick around all four edges of the cookie square and a dab on each end of two of the cookie strips. Referring to illustration C, press the sides of the basket in

ILLUSTRATION C

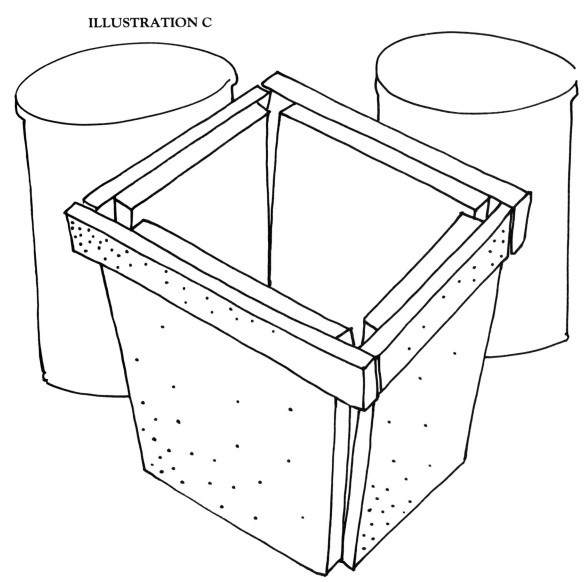

place so that the frosting holds the pieces together—it will be easiest to attach two adjoining sides first, support them with the cans or jars, and then add the remaining two sides, supporting them with two more cans or jars. To give the basket added strength, use some of the remaining frosting to apply a line inside the basket along the bottom piece where each side section is attached. Repeat the procedure with the remaining basket pieces. Allow both baskets to dry until the frosting is hard, at least 3 hours or as long as overnight.

6. Glaze the berries: Leaving the hulls intact, rinse the strawberries and let them dry. Place the jelly in a small saucepan set over medium heat and, stirring frequently, heat it until it has melted and is simmering. Holding one berry at a time by its stem and tilting the pan if necessary, immerse each berry in the glaze; place on a plate or cookie sheet. Continue until all are glazed, reheating the jelly if it begins to set in the pan. Refrigerate the berries until the jelly has set, about 15 minutes.

7. Assemble and serve the baskets: Reserving some of the most attractive strawberries, pile the remaining berries into the two baskets. Top with the reserved berries. To serve after the baskets have been displayed, break the sides away and place one on each plate; spoon the glazed berries over the cookie and serve with the whipped cream.

Pickled Vegetable Antipasto Jars

(Photograph on page 92)

Besides being surprisingly attractive in glass jars, this myriad of marinated vegetables also makes a delicious addition to any antipasto assortment. Arranging the vegetables into jars is a kitchen craft that allows you to be as artistic as you like. All that you have to do is cut the colorful vegetables into fanciful shapes, arrange them in decorative designs and borders, and marinate them in a zesty, herbed pickling solution.

The vegetable antipasto jars are quickly pickled and do not require the traditional preserving procedure that sealed jars do. However, these vegetables should be kept tightly covered in the refrigerator and eaten within two weeks.

A beautiful antipasto jar would make a great housewarming gift or colorful centerpiece at an Italian supper. Serve the antipasto with a slotted spoon and drizzle the vegetables with the best green olive oil you can find.

Pickled Vegetable Antipasto Jars

Specific quantities for the vegetables used to make these antipasto jars have not been given because you might want to combine yours in different ways. Keep in mind that the jar (or jars) you choose must have an opening large enough to allow for your hand to position the vegetables, although chopsticks or wooden dowels are also helpful for this job, and that it must have a tight-fitting lid. If you choose a 2-quart jar, you will need 2 quarts (packed) of vegetables. I usually pack the center of the jar with chopped cabbage, carrot slices, broccoli, and other vegetables left after I have cut the designs that will show through the glass.

The Pickling Solution:
2½ cups dry white wine
1½ cups distilled white vinegar
 ¼ cup sherry vinegar or cider
   vinegar
 2 tablespoons salt
 ¼ cup sugar
 1 tablespoon dried basil
 1 teaspoon dried oregano
 1 teaspoon peppercorns, coarsely
   cracked
 2 garlic cloves, sliced
 1 bay leaf
 1 to 2 dried hot red chili peppers
   (optional)
   additional salt and distilled
   vinegar

Vegetables to be Blanched:
  broccoli
  green beans
  yellow wax beans
  fresh, shelled peas

  fresh, shelled lima beans
  baby eggplants
  baby artichokes
  mushrooms
  Japanese enoki mushrooms

Vegetables to be Salted:
  red or green bell peppers
  pickling cucumbers, such as kirbys
  carrots
  celery
  green cabbage
  white turnips

Preserved Vegetables:
  pimiento-stuffed green olives
  small unpitted green olives
  Greek-style black olives

Accompaniments:
  extra-virgin olive oil
  prosciutto and/or salami
  sliced Provolone and/or mozzarella
  deviled eggs

1. Prepare the pickling solution: In a large, noncorrosive saucepan, combine the wine, white vinegar, sherry vinegar, 2 tablespoons salt, the sugar, basil, oregano, pepper, garlic, bay leaf, and chili peppers. Place the pan over moderately high heat and bring to a boil. Remove from the heat and let rest while you prepare the vegetables. Bring back to a boil just before adding the vegetables.

2. Blanch the vegetables to be partially cooked: Bring a large pot of water to a boil over high heat and add 1 tablespoon of salt for every 2 quarts of water. The timing below is based on the time that the boiling resumes after the vegetables have been added. Blanch one variety of vegetable at a time, remove it, and then proceed with another variety. After placing the vegetables in pickling solution or distilled vinegar, allow them to marinate for about 2 hours.

Broccoli, sliced through the stem ¼ inch thick . . . . . 2 minutes
   (remove with a slotted spoon and place in the pan of hot
   pickling solution)
Green and yellow wax beans . . . . 3 minutes
   (remove with a slotted spoon and place in the pan of hot
   pickling solution)
Fresh, shelled peas . . . . 2 minutes
   (remove with a slotted spoon and place in the pan of hot
   pickling solution)
Fresh, shelled lima beans . . . . 3 minutes
   (remove with a slotted spoon, place in a small noncorrosive
   bowl, and cover with distilled white vinegar)

Baby eggplants, stems removed, split lengthwise .... 3 minutes
(remove with a slotted spoon and place in the pan of hot
pickling solution)

Baby artichokes .... about 15 minutes
(slice in half lengthwise and place in the pan of hot pickling
solution)

Mushrooms, sliced ¼ inch thick .... 30 seconds
(remove with a slotted spoon and place in a small bowl;
cover with distilled white vinegar)

Japanese *enoki* mushrooms .... 2 seconds
(place on a slotted spoon and dip into boiling water; place in a
bowl and cover with distilled white vinegar)

3. Prepare the vegetables to be salted: Depending on the design you wish to make, cut the following vegetables into the desired shapes: bell peppers, pickling cucumbers, carrots, celery, cabbage, and turnips. For flowers or hearts that need special shapes to fit between them (see illus. A-1, A-2, and A-3), leave

ILLUSTRATION A-1

ILLUSTRATION A-3

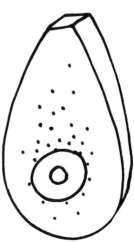

ILLUSTRATION A-2

the vegetables in pieces large enough to be cut after the salting process. In a separate bowl, you might combine chopped cabbage, sliced carrots, and vegetable trimmings to pack the center of the jar; this mixture will hold the designs pressed against the glass. Toss each 2 cups of uncooked vegetable pieces in a large bowl with 2 teaspoons salt. Let rest at room temperature for 2 hours, tossing occasionally.

4. To assemble the jar(s): Have ready a clean jar(s) with an opening large enough that your hand will fit through and chopsticks or two lengths of wooden doweling to help position the vegetables as you work. Reserving the liquid, carefully remove the vegetables from the pickling solution with a slotted spoon, placing each variety on a separate plate. Drain the vegetables that were soaked in the distilled vinegar and discard the vinegar. Place each variety on a separate plate. Rinse those tossed with salt, drain in a colander, and place on separate plates. Slice the pimiento-stuffed green olives crosswise and incorporate them in the designs along with the black and unpitted green olives. Notice that each jar in the color photograph has been designed in bands of vegetables, so begin by placing a band around the bottom, pressing the vegetables against the glass (see illus. B). Then pack the center tightly with additional salted or pickled

ILLUSTRATION B

vegetables to hold the designs in place. Continue adding bands and packing the center until the jar is full and very tightly packed (if you have not packed it tightly enough, the vegetables will rise to the surface and ruin your design). Cover the vegetables with the reserved pickling solution. Cover and refrigerate.

5. To serve, remove the desired vegetables with a slotted spoon and place on individual plates. Drizzle the antipasto with the olive oil and, to make the antipasto assortment complete, serve with prosciutto, salami, Provolone, mozzarella, and deviled eggs.

4
Main Courses

Standing Rib Roast with Potato-Chip Roses

The standing rib roast is most frequently reserved for special occasions, and considering its high price tag these days, rightfully so. At its best, it is juicy pink, tender, and succulent. If you want to make it look extra-special, adorn the platter with a garland of crisp Potato-Chip Roses in full bloom.

The almost-lost art of making Potato-Chip Roses seems limited to an occasional banquet served at an expensive hotel or on an ocean liner. True, making the flowers does take some practice, patience, and a sharp vegetable slicer or knife, but, once you get the knack of it, you'll be able to turn them out by the dozen. After they have been shaped, they can be kept in cold water until you are ready to deep-fry them. When they have cooled, they'll remain crisp overnight if placed in an airtight container. You'll find this delicious, golden garnish a welcome addition to your repertoire and certainly a worthy accompaniment to any standing rib roast.

Standing Rib Roast

Since this tender, juicy cut of beef takes quite a while to roast, you can make the Potato-Chip Roses to garnish the platter while it cooks.
8 TO 10 SERVINGS

4-rib roast (prime ribs), trimmed
  and tied to yield about 9 pounds
  (see Note), preferably cut from the
  first four ribs
1 tablespoon vegetable oil
4 large garlic cloves, each cut into
  10 slivers, or 2 teaspoons of your

favorite herb
2 tablespoons all-purpose flour
1 teaspoon freshly ground pepper
  salt to taste
  Potato-Chip Roses (instructions
  follow)
  watercress or parsley for garnish

Note: Have your butcher remove the chine bone, trim off any excess fat, and tie the roast.

1. Preheat the oven to 450°F. Choose a roasting pan just slightly larger than the roast (no rack is necessary because the ribs form a natural rack). Rub the portion of the meat not covered with fat with the oil. If using the garlic, use the tip of a paring or boning knife to cut forty slits into the roast, evenly spacing the cuts; insert a sliver of garlic into each. In a small bowl, combine the flour and pepper. If you are omitting the garlic, add your favorite herb to the flour and pepper. Rub the mixture all over the roast and place it, bone side down, in the roasting pan.

2. Place the roast in the oven. Roast for 15 minutes, reduce the heat to 325°F., and continue roasting until done to your taste—about 15 minutes per pound for rare, 20 minutes per pound for medium, and about 25 minutes per pound for a well-done roast. On a meat thermometer, the temperature will be about 125°F. for rare, 140°F. for medium, and about 150°F. for a well-done roast.

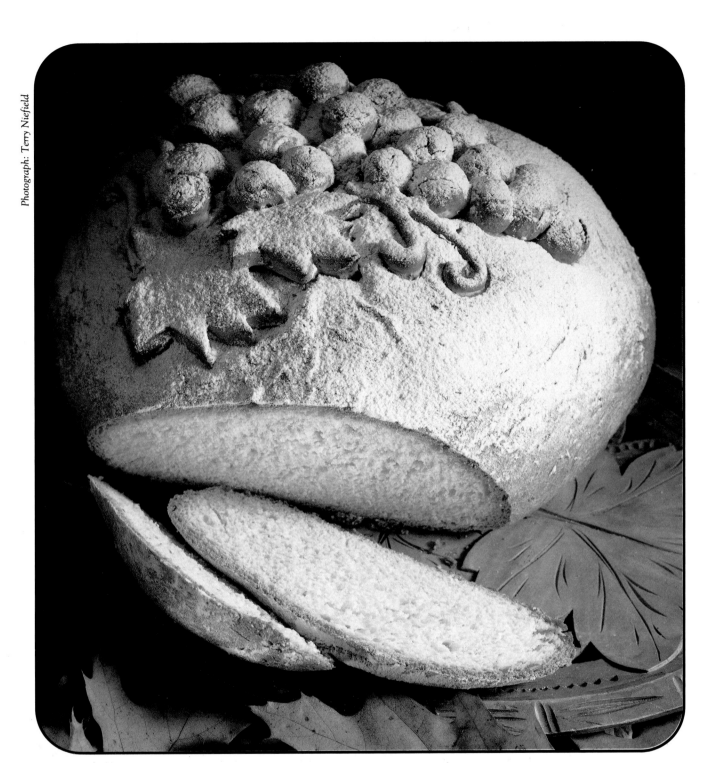

Bas-Relief Oat Bread, p. 38.

Above: *Mosaic Shrimp-and-Salmon Mousse*, p. 18.

Above: *Liquados (Fresh Fruit Drinks)*, p. 135.

Cornucopia with Cream Puffs and Chocolate Sauce, p. 168.

Pickled Vegetable Antipasto Jars, p. 83.

The Well-Dressed Turkey with Frosted Grapes, p. 151.

Sugar-Sifted Holiday Cookies and Brownies, p. 159.

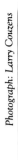

Lovely Layered Cheeses, p. 27.

Watermelon Wedges, p. 72.

Bread Basket with Daisy Rolls, p. 49.

Remove the roast from the oven, and let it rest for 15 to 20 minutes. Place it on a platter and garnish the platter with Potato-Chip Roses and the watercress or parsley. Serve hot or warm.

Potato-Chip Roses

To make Potato-Chip Roses, use one 8-ounce baking potato, either peeled or unpeeled, for every four roses desired. Using a vegetable slicer or a very sharp knife, cut the potatoes crosswise into slices about 1/16 inch. (If you use a knife, count on wasting some of the slices because it takes some practice to be able to cut the whole, even slices required.) For each rose that you want to make, pare down a 3-inch length of carrot to the diameter of a pencil.

To make one rose: Wrap one of the small slices of potato around a piece of carrot, holding it tightly at the base with your fingers (see illus. A).

ILLUSTRATION A

Then wrap another small slice around it so that the overlap is opposite that of the first slice (see illus. B). Add a third slice in the same way and then insert a

ILLUSTRATION B

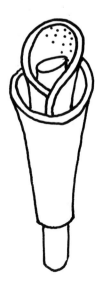

toothpick through the slices into the carrot to hold them in place (see illus. C). Continue adding potato slices until the rose is the size you wish, using more

ILLUSTRATION C

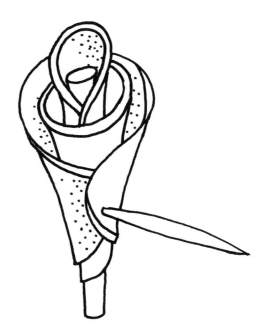

toothpicks as necessary (see illus. D). Each time you add another petal, remove the toothpicks and hold the petals in place with your fingers until you can reinsert them. As you complete each rose, place it in ice water. If refrigerated at this stage, the roses will hold for several hours.

ILLUSTRATION D

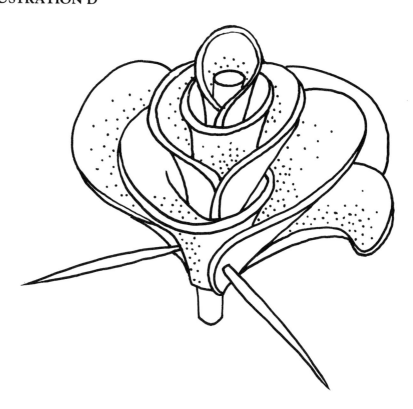

To fry the roses, place about 2½ inches of peanut oil in a deep-fat fryer or a tall, narrow, heavy saucepan that is at least twice as deep as the depth of oil to allow room for the oil to bubble up when adding the potatoes. Heat the oil to 375°F. on a deep-fat frying thermometer, almost to the smoking point. Meanwhile, pat the roses dry with paper towels, turn them upside down, and let them dry completely so that they won't splatter when added to the oil (to facilitate drying, you can use a fan or hair dryer). Place one rose on a slotted spoon and lower it into the hot oil. Fry the bottom of the rose for about 20 seconds and then, holding the extended portion of carrot with tongs, carefully turn the rose upside down and submerge the petals in the oil. Cook the rose until it is golden brown, 1½ to 2 minutes, turning it several times. If the oil begins to smoke, reduce the heat slightly. Remove the rose from the oil and drain it on paper towels. Continue frying and draining enough roses to garnish your platter. When they have cooled completely, carefully remove the toothpicks by gently twisting them out. Remove and discard the carrot from the bottom of the rose—the petals will adhere to each other.

Double-Glazed Chicken Breasts

Here, poached chicken breasts are chilled and coated with a variation of the classic French sauce *chaud-froid*. Opaque and creamy white in color, it makes a perfect "canvas" for a simple spring floral arrangement of scallion greens and pimiento rounds.

Don't let these suggestions dictate your own design ideas, however. You can use fresh peas and baby carrot slivers for your decorations, or you might want to try black olive slices with bell-pepper triangles. The design possibilities are limitless, so feel free to experiment with other ingredients.

After you have created the design, the chicken breasts are chilled and then coated with a layer of transparent White Wine Aspic. Serve the final dish as the main course at a special luncheon or buffet.

Double-Glazed Chicken Breasts

The chilled chicken breasts in this recipe will be coated a total of three times and possibly a fourth if the third application is too thin, so plan for several hours' preparation time.

8 SERVINGS

The Chicken and White Glaze:
8 *skinless, boneless chicken-breast halves of equal size (about 2 pounds)*
1⅔ *cups degreased chicken stock*
1 *cup dry white wine*
1 *cup heavy cream*
1 *large garlic clove, sliced crosswise*
1 *teaspoon dried tarragon*
1 *envelope (¼ ounce) unflavored gelatin*

salt to taste

Final Glaze:
White Wine Aspic (recipe follows)

Decorations (see Note):
scallion greens
1 *to 2 pimientos, rinsed and drained*

Optional Garnish:
stuffed cherry tomatoes

Note: Other vegetables can be substituted for the scallion greens and pimientos, such as pieces of carrot, green bean, red or green bell pepper, or peas and truffles.

1. To poach the chicken breasts: Trim away any fat and the tendon from the undersides of the chicken breasts. In a large, noncorrosive Dutch oven, skillet, or sauté pan, combine the chicken stock and wine. Add the chicken breasts, smooth sides up, and place the pan over low heat. Bring the liquid to a simmer, cover, and poach gently, turning the chicken several times, until just cooked through, about 10 minutes after the liquid has come to a simmer. To test for doneness, remove one breast from the liquid and cut into the center of the underside (nonsmooth side); it should no longer be pink. If it is still pink, return it to the liquid and poach until just done. Avoid overcooking the chicken, or it will be dry. Letting any excess liquid run back into the pan, transfer the chicken with tongs to one or two plates, cover with plastic wrap, cool to room temperature, and then refrigerate until chilled.

2. Meanwhile, prepare the White Glaze: To the liquid in the pan, add the cream, garlic, and tarragon. Bring the mixture to a boil over high heat, stirring frequently. (Depending on the pan you are using, it may be necessary to reduce the heat slightly to prevent boiling over.) Boil until reduced to 2 cups (measure in a heatproof measuring cup), 5 to 10 minutes. Meanwhile, place ¼ cup cold water in a medium-size, heatproof bowl and sprinkle the gelatin over it; stir until blended and let rest.

3. When the liquid has reduced to 2 cups, pour it over the gelatin mixture and stir to dissolve the gelatin. Cool to room temperature, stirring occasionally. If a layer of fat forms on the top, quickly blot it with a paper towel (a small amount of fat remaining is all right). Meanwhile, prepare the White Wine Aspic and cut out the vegetable decorations (see step 4) while the aspic is cooling to room temperature.

4. Prepare the decorations: Referring to the following designs or creating your own, cut the vegetables into flowers and stems or other decorative shapes (I used pimientos for the flowers and scallions for stems). Set the shapes on a plate, cover with plastic wrap, and refrigerate until needed.

5. When the White Glaze has cooled to room temperature, taste it for seasoning; add a little salt if necessary. Chill the glaze, stirring frequently, until it has the consistency of thick, smooth syrup—you can do this in the refrigerator or over a bowl of ice. If the glaze should set before you coat the chicken breasts, heat it gently over a bowl or pan of hot water, stirring, only until it has melted; then chill it again to the consistency of syrup.

6. Glaze the chicken: Place the breasts smooth side up on your work surface and trim away any ragged edges. Place the breasts, again smooth side up, on a plate or platter. Spoon about 2 tablespoons of the glaze over each breast half to coat evenly. Refrigerate until the glaze has set. (Leave the remaining glaze at room temperature so that it does not set.) Remove the chicken from the

ILLUSTRATION A

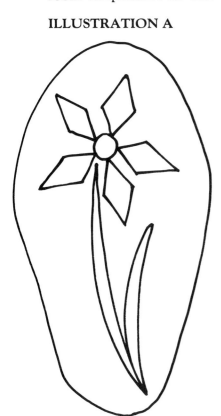

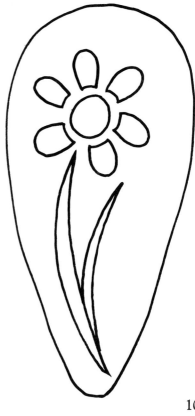

refrigerator, and, using a paring knife, cut away any of the glaze on the plate around each breast half to make a neat shape. Then glaze as before. Referring to the preceding illustrations, apply the desired designs. Refrigerate until the glaze has set.

7. Meanwhile, stirring frequently, chill the White Wine Aspic either in the refrigerator or over a bowl of ice until it has the consistency of a thick, smooth syrup. After the second coating of White Glaze has set, remove the chicken from the refrigerator. Again, trim the glaze around each breast half, place the breasts on a clean plate, and spoon the White Wine Aspic over them to coat evenly. Refrigerate until the aspic has set. Apply a second coating if the first application was too thin or uneven and chill until set.

8. To serve: Trim the aspic around each breast half and arrange the chicken on a serving platter in a radial design. Garnish with stuffed cherry tomatoes if desired. Serve cold.

White Wine Aspic

This jewellike, transparent aspic can be used to glaze canapés and pâtés or poured into a shallow pan and cut into tiny cubes to garnish an elegant dish. Here, it is used as a glaze over the beautifully decorated Double-Glazed Chicken Breasts. If you are using this aspic in another recipe, you might want to substitute another dried herb for the tarragon.

MAKES ABOUT 2 CUPS

1⅔ cups degreased chicken stock
 ½ cup dry white wine
⅓ cup chopped onion
 ½ teaspoon dried tarragon
 1 tablespoon white wine vinegar or distilled white vinegar

1 envelope (¼ ounce) unflavored gelatin
1 egg (you will need the egg white and shell only)
salt if necessary

1. In a small, heavy, noncorrosive saucepan, combine the chicken stock, wine, onion, tarragon, and vinegar. Sprinkle the gelatin over the top and then stir it in.

2. Separate the egg and, reserving the yolk for another use, add the egg white to the pan. Crush the shell in your hands and add it to the pan.

3. Place the pan over low heat and, stirring frequently, bring the mixture just to a boil. Reduce the heat to an even lower temperature and, without stirring, keep the mixture at a bare simmer without disturbing it for 15 minutes.

4. Meanwhile, cut four layers of cheesecloth that will fit into a strainer or colander; run them under water and then wring out so that the cloth is damp; line the strainer with the cheesecloth. Place the strainer over a bowl. Carefully ladle the contents of the pan into the prepared strainer; the aspic should be perfectly clear. Cool to room temperature.

Salad-Filled Pies

(Photograph on page 8)

To look at this lattice-topped pie is to fool the eye. It appears to contain a filling that has been baked inside the crust, while, in reality, the pie shell is baked separately from the lattice top. The pie shown in the photo is filled with a chilled Shrimp-Salad Filling and then the crisp top placed over it. To give the dressing that binds it a delicious consistency, hard-cooked eggs have been puréed into it. Because shrimp prices continue to skyrocket, three alternative recipes have been included here that can fill the shell as well.

I cannot recommend my favorite filling to you because I like all of them. The Mushroom-Salad Filling is chockful of mushrooms that have been cooked in white wine and then enhanced with a bit of blue cheese, while the Chicken Salad is flavored with cumin and chopped walnuts. To create the Layered Ham, Spinach, and Cheese-Filled Pie, you begin by lining a shell with slices of Provolone and topping them with a hot, freshly cooked spinach layer, which melts the cheese onto the crust. Once the heat is gone, cool ham salad is spread over the spinach and the whole is topped with the latticework.

Serve these savory main-dish pies at informal luncheons, picnics, or buffets along with marinated vegetables and a green salad. Fresh fruit should be all that you need to round out the menu.

Mushroom-Salad Filling
MAKES ENOUGH TO FILL ONE 9-INCH PIE

2 cups plus 1 tablespoon dry white wine
2 pounds small, whole mushrooms (quarter if large), wiped clean and ¼ inch of stems removed
¾ cup sour cream

2 ounces finely crumbled blue cheese
salt and freshly ground pepper to taste
1 9-inch baked Butter Pastry Shell and Lattice Top (recipe follows)

1. Place 2 cups of the wine in a large, noncorrosive pot set over high heat and bring to a boil; add the mushrooms and cook, stirring occasionally, for 15 minutes. Strain, reserving the juices (you should have about 1¾ cups); let the mushrooms cool to room temperature.

2. Place the mushroom liquid in a small, heavy pan and boil over moderately high heat until reduced to 3 tablespoons, about 10 minutes; reserve.

3. Place the mushrooms in a large bowl and toss well with the sour cream, blue cheese, remaining 1 tablespoon white wine, salt and pepper to taste, and the reserved mushroom glaze.

4. Place the filling in the pie shell, spreading it so that it is even with the top of the crust. Carefully slide the lattice top off the cookie sheet onto the filling and center it. If the lattice sticks to the sheet, place the cookie sheet directly over a burner set at moderate heat for a moment or two, or until it loosens. Wrap the pie in plastic wrap and chill until ready to serve. Let rest about 15 minutes at room temperature before serving. Cut into wedges and serve cold.

Layered Ham, Spinach, and Cheese Filling
MAKES ENOUGH TO FILL ONE 9-INCH PIE

about 1 pound of cooked ham, cut into ¼-inch dice (2 cups)
¼ cup Basic Mayonnaise (see recipe, p. 25)
¼ cup sour cream
2 tablespoons Dijon-style mustard
1 tablespoon olive oil
1 medium-size onion, chopped (1 cup)
1 cup (packed) cooked, chopped drained fresh spinach, (about 1 pound), or one package (10 ounces) frozen, chopped spinach, thawed
¼ teaspoon freshly ground nutmeg
¼ teaspoon salt
½ teaspoon freshly ground pepper
1 package (3 ounces) cream cheese
2 teaspoons fresh lemon juice
8 thin slices (4-inch rounds) Provolone cheese (6 ounces)
1 9-inch baked Butter Pastry Shell and Lattice Top (recipe follows)

1. In a medium-size bowl, combine the ham, Basic Mayonnaise, sour cream, and mustard; toss to blend, cover, and refrigerate until needed.

2. Place the oil in a medium-size skillet set over moderate heat; add the onion and sauté until soft and translucent, about 5 minutes. Add the spinach, nutmeg, salt, and pepper; cook, stirring frequently, for about 3 minutes, or until the spinach is hot; remove from the heat and stir in the cream cheese until melted. Stir in the lemon juice.

3. Overlap four slices of the Provolone over the bottom of the baked shell. Spread the spinach filling over the cheese; top with the remaining Provolone, and let cool for 10 minutes. Spread enough of the ham filling over the cheese to make the filling just even with the top of the shell. Top with a grinding of pepper. Carefully slide the lattice top from the cookie sheet onto the filling and center it. If it sticks to the sheet, place the cookie sheet directly over a burner set at moderate heat for a moment or two, or until it loosens. Cover the pie with plastic wrap and refrigerate. Allow to rest at room temperature for 15 minutes before serving. Cut into wedges and serve.

Chicken-Salad Filling
MAKES ENOUGH TO FILL ONE 9-INCH PIE

1½ pounds skinless, boneless chicken breasts, halved lengthwise
1 cup finely diced celery
½ cup sliced scallions
½ cup chopped walnuts
1 teaspoon ground cumin
½ teaspoon salt
¼ teaspoon freshly ground pepper
½ cup Basic Mayonnaise (see recipe, p. 25)
½ cup sour cream
1 jar (4 ounces) pimientos, rinsed, drained, and cut into ¼-inch pieces
1 9-inch baked Butter Pastry Shell and Lattice Top (recipe follows)

1. Place the chicken breasts and 3 cups cold water in a medium-size saucepan over moderate heat; when the water simmers, reduce the heat to low and simmer the breasts until just done, 10 to 15 minutes; when cut into, they should be opaque throughout. Let them cool in the water to room temperature.

2. Cut the chicken into ¾-inch cubes and place them in a large bowl along with the celery, scallions, walnuts, cumin, salt, and pepper. Stir in the Basic Mayonnaise and sour cream, tossing to coat the chicken. Gently stir in the pimientos.

3. Scoop the filling into the pastry shell, spreading it so that it is even with the top edge of the pie shell. Carefully slide the lattice top off the cookie sheet onto the filling and center it. If the lattice top sticks to the sheet, place the cookie sheet directly over a burner set at moderate heat for a moment or two, or until it loosens. Wrap the pie in plastic wrap and chill until ready to serve. Let rest at room temperature 15 minutes before serving. Cut into wedges and serve.

Shrimp-Salad Filling
MAKES ENOUGH TO FILL ONE 9-INCH PIE

2 pounds medium-size shrimp,
 shelled, deveined, and cooked
½ teaspoon salt
2 hard-cooked eggs, chopped
⅓ cup Basic Mayonnaise (see recipe,
 p. 25)
¼ cup sour cream

2 teaspoons Dijon-style mustard
½ cup thinly sliced scallions
¼ cup (packed) minced parsley
2 tablespoons fresh lemon juice
 freshly ground pepper to taste
1 9-inch baked Butter Pastry Shell
 and Lattice Top (recipe follows)

1. In a blender or food processor, combine one-fourth of the shrimp, the salt, eggs, Basic Mayonnaise, sour cream, and mustard; blend until smooth.

2. Cut the remaining shrimp into ½-inch pieces and place them in a large bowl along with the scallions, parsley, and lemon juice. Add the dressing from step 1, toss well, and add pepper to taste.

3. Place the filling in the pie shell, spreading it so that it is even with the top of the crust. Carefully slide the lattice top off the cookie sheet onto the filling and center it. If the lattice sticks to the cookie sheet, place it directly over a burner set at moderate heat for a moment or two, or until it loosens. Wrap the pie in plastic wrap and chill until ready to serve. Let rest at room temperature for about 15 minutes before serving. Cut into wedges and serve.

Butter Pastry for Shells and Lattice Tops
MAKES ONE 9-INCH SHELL AND LATTICE TOP

2 cups all-purpose flour
½ teaspoon salt
8 tablespoons (1 stick) unsalted
  butter, chilled and thinly sliced

3 tablespoons vegetable shortening
¼ cup plus 1 tablespoon ice water
  egg yolk for glaze

1. Make the butter pastry: In a large mixing bowl, combine the flour and salt. Cut in the butter and shortening until the mixture resembles coarse meal. Sprinkle the top with ¼ cup of the ice water; stir rapidly with a fork, adding enough drops of the remaining water so that the dough can be gathered loosely into a ball. Flatten it gently, wrap tightly, and refrigerate for about 2 hours or overnight.

2. Prepare the pie shell: Preheat the oven to 425°F. Lightly oil a cookie sheet (without edges) and dust it with flour, tapping out the excess. Invert a 9-inch pie pan in the center and trace a line around it, using a knife tip. Remove the pie pan and reserve the baking sheet. Remove two-thirds of the dough from the refrigerator, rewrapping the remainder and refrigerating it. Quickly shape the dough into a flat round and, on a lightly floured surface with a lightly floured rolling pin, roll it ⅛ inch thick. Without stretching it, loosely drape it into the 9-inch pie pan. Using a sharp knife, trim the dough flush with the pie pan all around. Carefully line the pastry with aluminum foil, fill it with dried beans or pie weights, and bake in the center of the oven for 12 to 15 minutes, or until the edge of the pastry has set all around and is beginning to brown slightly. Remove the foil and beans or weights, return the pie shell to the oven, and bake until crisp and golden brown, about 5 minutes. If the bottom should bubble up during the final baking, prick it with a fork until it lies flat. Cool the shell, still in the pan, on a wire rack to room temperature.

3. Prepare the lattice top: On a lightly floured surface, roll out the remaining pastry to about a ⅛-inch-thick (or slightly more) square that measures 12 by 12 inches. Using a pastry wheel with a crimped edge or a knife and ruler, cut the pastry into strips ½ inch wide or slightly wider. Place six strips of the pastry, leaving about ¾ inch between each, parallel to each other over the circle you traced onto the baking sheet. Fold the first, third, and fifth strips in half back over themselves. Lay a seventh strip horizontally across the center of the unfolded strips so that it just touches the folds of the others (see illus. A). Unfold the folded strips (see illus. B) and fold back the second, fourth, and sixth strips ¾ inch away from the horizontal strip just placed (see illus. C). Lay another strip across the unfolded strips and just touching the folds of the others. In the same way, weave in a third strip. Turn the lattice top around and weave in three more crosswise strips in the same way. Trim the ends of each strip evenly to make a 9-inch circle.

4. In a small bowl, lightly beat together the egg yolk with 1 teaspoon cold water. Using a pastry brush, paint the entire top of the lattice with the glaze. Using as many of the remaining strips of pastry as necessary, frame the lattice circle by attaching the strips to the top of the outer edge all around (see illus. D); press gently so that the strips adhere to the glaze. When it is necessary to add another strip of pastry, overlap one of its ends over the end of the last strip, smooth it to blend, and continue framing. Brush the framing with more of the glaze. Bake the lattice in the center of the oven for about 12 minutes, or until it is crisp and golden brown. Cool directly on the baking sheet placed on a rack.

ILLUSTRATION A

ILLUSTRATION B

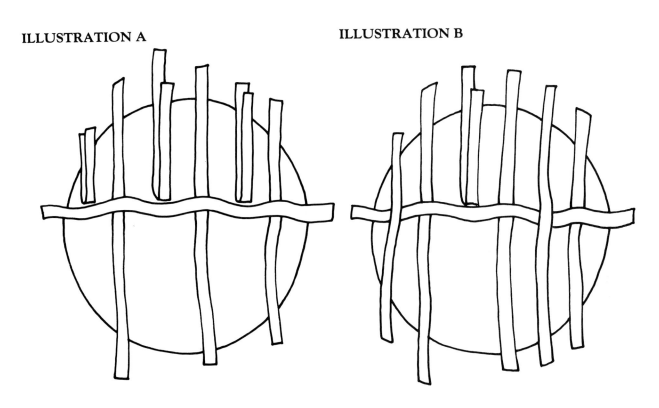

ILLUSTRATION C

ILLUSTRATION D

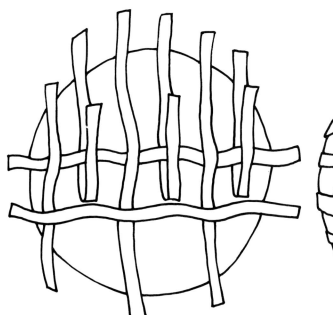

Glazed Red Snapper with Cucumber Chain

Although this classic cold buffet presentation is traditionally made with a fresh, whole poached salmon, I have chosen to use a red snapper because it has a glowing, pinkish coral color and a wonderful, delicate flavor. To represent the scales of the fish, thin slices of cucumber are arranged over it in an overlapping pattern and the whole is then glazed with transparent aspic. For embellishment, fancy borders of mayonnaise are piped around the face. Finally, the edge of the platter is garnished all around with an easily made cucumber chain or deviled eggs.

You can serve this edible work of art as the cold portion of an elegant buffet or as the main course of a cool, summer dinner.

Glazed Red Snapper

To make this recipe, you will need a large, enameled roasting pan with a flat rack that is large enough to hold the fish yet small enough to fit into your refrigerator.

8 TO 10 SERVINGS

3 quarts Basic Fish Stock (recipe
   follows)
4- to 5-pound whole, fresh red
   snapper
2 medium-size cucumbers, peeled
2 teaspoons salt
4 cups Aspic Glaze (recipe follows)

¼ cup mayonnaise

Optional Garnishes:
   Cucumber Chain (instructions
   follow) or deviled-egg halves
   topped with pitted black-olive
   slices
1 black-olive slice for eye of fish
   round cutouts of pimiento

1. Place the Basic Fish Stock in an enameled roasting pan large enough to hold the fish and bring it to a boil. Using a ruler, measure the snapper at its thickest point; poaching time will be 10 minutes for every 1 inch of thickness (this time guide is for all types of fish). For example, if your fish is 3 inches thick, it should poach for 30 minutes. Place the snapper on a flat rack and lower it into the boiling stock. Reduce the heat so that the stock is at a simmer, cover the pan, and poach according to the above time schedule. Reserving the stock to make the Aspic Glaze, remove the fish, still on the rack, cover it loosely with aluminum foil, and cool to room temperature. Then, remove the skin on one side from the gills to the tail (this will become the top side), using a paring knife to pull it off. Cover the fish loosely with aluminum foil and refrigerate until chilled.

2. Meanwhile, prepare the Aspic Glaze and chill it to syrupy consistency. Then pour as much of it as is necessary over a serving platter to coat it with ¼ inch of aspic; chill the platter until the aspic has set. Reserve the remaining aspic at room temperature.

3. When the fish is chilled, slice the cucumbers as thinly as possible, place them in a bowl, and toss with the salt. Let the slices rest for 20 minutes, rinse, and then drain the slices. Pat them dry before using.

4. Slide the chilled snapper onto the center of the aspic-coated platter. Beginning with the smallest slices of cucumber, dip each into the syrupy aspic, and then, beginning at the tail end of the fish, arrange them in an overlapping pattern to resemble the scales of a fish (see illus. A). Continue adding slices until you reach the gill and then trim them to the shape of the fish head. Refrigerate until the aspic has set. Spoon enough of the remaining syrupy aspic over the fish to coat the fish and cucumber "scales" evenly. Refrigerate until the aspic has set. If the coating is too thin or uneven, spoon a third layer over it.

ILLUSTRATION A

5. Fit a pastry bag with a small, plain tip, ⅛ inch wide or less, and fill it with the mayonnaise. Referring to illustration A, pipe a border design along the line that defines the fish head. Pipe flower-petal shapes around the eye. Top the eye with a slice of black olive if desired. Garnish the edge of the platter all around with the optional Cucumber Chain or deviled eggs, each topped with a slice of black olive. For added color, add rounds of pimiento if desired. Serve chilled.

Basic Fish Stock

This basic stock is the poaching stock for the red snapper in this recipe, although it lends itself to poaching other fish as well. The fish heads and bones required can usually be obtained from your fish market for the asking or a small fee.

MAKES ABOUT 3 QUARTS

3 pounds fish bones and heads from
    nonoily fish, such as halibut,
    haddock, sole, or flounder
3 sprigs of parsley
1 bay leaf

1 teaspoon dried thyme
6 peppercorns, coarsely cracked
1 large onion, sliced
3 ribs celery, coarsely chopped
1 cup dry white wine

1. In a large bowl, soak the fish bones and heads in cold water to cover for 20 minutes. Strain them through a colander, rinsing them well to remove any traces of blood; remove and discard the gills from the fish heads.

2. In a large, heavy stockpot or Dutch oven, place the fish bones and heads along with 3½ quarts of cold water. Make a *bouquet garni* by placing the parsley, bay leaf, thyme, and pepper on a square of cheesecloth and tie it into a bundle. Add the *bouquet garni* to the stockpot along with the onion, celery, and wine. Place the pot over moderately high heat and bring the mixture to a boil. Reduce the heat to low and simmer for 30 minutes.

3. Place a large strainer or colander lined with several layers of damp cheesecloth over a large, enameled roasting pan and strain the stock through it, discarding the solids. The stock is now ready to use or it may be cooled to room temperature and refrigerated.

Aspic Glaze

MAKES ABOUT 4 CUPS

3 quarts Basic Fish Stock (recipe
    precedes)
2 envelopes (¼ ounce each)

unflavored gelatin
3 eggs (whites and shells only)
salt to taste

1. Bring the stock to a boil over high heat. Boil it rapidly, reducing the heat only if necessary to prevent it from boiling over, until the stock has reduced to 4 cups, about 30 minutes, depending on the pan that you are using.

2. Place ½ cup cold water in a small, heatproof bowl and sprinkle the gelatin over the top; stir to soften and then let it rest for 3 minutes. Stir the gelatin into the hot stock mixture until the gelatin melts. Let the mixture cool to room temperature and then transfer it to a heavy, medium-size saucepan.

3. Using a whisk or a fork, stir in the egg whites; crush the eggshells and add them also. Place the pan over low heat and, stirring frequently, bring the mixture just to a boil. Reduce the heat to an even lower temperature and, without stirring or disturbing, barely simmer the mixture for 15 minutes.

4. To clarify the aspic, line a strainer or colander with four layers of dampened cheesecloth. Place the strainer over a heatproof bowl and carefully ladle the contents of the pan through the prepared strainer. The aspic should be transparent. Cool to room temperature, taste for seasoning, and add salt if necessary.

5. Before glazing the red snapper, chill the aspic until it has the consistency of thick, smooth syrup. You can do this, stirring frequently, either in the refrigerator or over a bowl of ice water. If your aspic should set before you have a chance to use it, heat it gently over a bowl or pan of hot water, stirring it only until it has melted; then repeat the chilling procedure until the aspic has the consistency of syrup. To avoid its setting, keep it at room temperature.

Cucumber Chain

Peel three 7-inch-long cucumbers, trim the ends, and cut the cucumbers into 2-inch lengths (see illus. B-1). Using a coring tool or a small spoon, scoop out

ILLUSTRATION B-1

the seeds from the center of each (see illus. B-2); then cut the cylinders into rings

ILLUSTRATION B-2

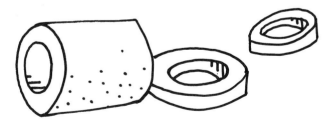

about ¼ inch thick. Using a paring knife, cut a slit through one half of each ring (see illus. B-3). To form the chain, pull open the slit of one ring and push

ILLUSTRATION B-3

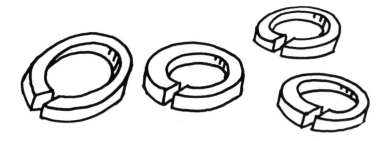

another ring through it (see illus. B-4). Continue adding rings in this way until the chain is long enough to go around the circumference of your platter.

ILLUSTRATION B-4

Glazed Lobster with Saffron-Lobster Salad

(Photograph on page 7)

In this recipe, medallions of lobster meat have been arranged over a saffron-lobster salad that has been mounded between the shiny red claws of a glazed lobster. The medallions have then been decorated with bits of red and green vegetables to complete the dramatic presentation—a dinner destined for a special occasion. Not only is the culinary display beautiful to look at, but the dish can be made hours ahead of time; in fact, it must be assembled in advance to allow enough time for it to chill completely before it is served. If you include the lobster platter as part of a buffet assortment, it will serve twice as many people.

Glazed Lobster with Saffron-Lobster Salad

To make this recipe, you will need an oval platter, 12 to 14 inches in diameter, that will fit into your refrigerator. You can make the fish stock required for the aspic a day ahead of time and keep it refrigerated until needed.

4 TO 6 SERVINGS

4 live lobsters (1½ to 1¾ pounds each)
2 cups Aspic Glaze (half the recipe for Aspic Glaze, see p. 110)
½ cup long-grain rice
1 tablespoon olive oil
2 grams saffron (¼ teaspoon crumbled or ½ teaspoon threads)
2 medium-size carrots, peeled and cut into ¼ inch dice (⅔ cup)
2 cups freshly shelled peas or one package (10 ounces) frozen peas

3 tablespoons thinly sliced scallions (3 to 4 small)
¼ cup minced parsley leaves
¼ cup mayonnaise
2 hard-cooked egg yolks, sieved
¼ teaspoon freshly ground pepper roe and tomally from lobsters (optional)
salt to taste
1 jar (4 ounces) pimientos, rinsed, drained, cut into rounds about ¼ inch in diameter, for decoration

1. Bring a large, deep kettle of water to a full, rolling boil over high heat and plunge one lobster in, head first. Keep the heat on high until the water returns to a boil and then reduce it so that it is simmering; partially cover the kettle and simmer for 8 to 10 minutes, depending on the size of lobster. Immediately remove the lobster with tongs, rinse under cold running water, and place on a large platter to drain and cool. Return the water to a boil and repeat the procedure with the remaining lobsters. When they have all cooled to room temperature, cover them and refrigerate until well chilled.

2. Meanwhile, make the Aspic Glaze and cool it to room temperature.

3. Place 2 quarts of water in a heavy, 3-quart saucepan and bring it to a boil over high heat. Add the rice to the water slowly enough that the boiling does not stop. Then boil the rice, uncovered, until tender but still firm to the bite, about 12 minutes (reduce the heat if necessary to prevent the water from boiling over but not so much that the boiling is not steady). Pour the rice through a strainer, rinse under cold running water, and dry it by shaking the strainer up and down and back and forth. Transfer it to a medium-size mixing bowl and toss it with the olive oil.

4. Place the saffron in a small, heatproof bowl and pour over it 1 tablespoon of boiling water; let it soak for 5 minutes, stirring occasionally, and then stir it into the rice. Set it aside.

5. Half-fill a medium-size saucepan with water and bring it to a boil over high heat. Drop in the carrots and cook until just tender but still slightly firm to the bite, about 3 minutes after the boiling resumes; reduce the heat slightly if necessary to prevent the water from boiling over. Strain the carrots through a wire sieve, rinse under cold running water, and place in a single layer on paper towels to dry. Then toss them with the rice.

6. Half-fill a medium-size saucepan with water and bring it to a boil over high heat. Drop in the peas and, after the boiling resumes, cook until just tender to the bite, 3 to 4 minutes for fresh peas or about 1 minute for frozen peas. Strain, rinse under cold running water, and then add 1 cup to the rice; reserve the remainder, covered, for decoration.

7. Toss the scallions, parsley, mayonnaise, egg yolks, and pepper with the rice mixture.

8. When chilled, remove the lobsters from the refrigerator. Reserving the best-looking lobster for the final presentation, break off the tail portions from the remaining three, using a knife to cut through if necessary. Using poultry shears and working on the underside of the three lobster tails, cut lengthwise through the bottom shell, cutting along both edges but not cutting into the lobster-tail meat; remove the bottom shell and gently pull out the tail meat in one piece. Using the same procedure with the whole lobster that you have reserved for the final presentation, carefully remove the tail meat without detaching the tail from the body. Rinse the carcass, drain it, and then chill it until needed. Place the four shelled lobster tails on a plate, cover, and chill until needed. Working with the three lobster carcasses, break off the main legs with the large claws still attached. Using poultry shears, cut into the claws and legs, remove all the meat, cut it into ½-inch pieces (you should have about 1 cup packed), and add it to the rice mixture. If you wish to use the pale green tomally and red roe (if present) in the salad, split the three carcasses in half lengthwise with a heavy cleaver or knife and remove. Add one or both to the rice mixture. To complete the salad, add salt to taste. Cover and chill until needed. (You may want to reserve the lobster carcasses and their drippings to make a rich stock.)

9. Referring to the photograph, mound the salad 4 to 5 inches high in the center at one end of an oval serving platter. Cut each of the four sections of lobster-tail meat into six crosswise slices (each about ¾ inch thick) to make medallions, reserving the two most attractive medallions to top the salad. One at a time, dip ten of the remaining medallions into aspic that has chilled to a syrupy consistency and arrange them around the outer edge of the salad, pushing them into the salad as you work. Add an inner circle of eight medallions dipped in aspic, and then finish with a final inside circle of four medallions. Dip the two reserved medallions into aspic glaze and center on top. Chill the platter until the aspic has set.

10. Meanwhile, place the whole chilled lobster carcass on a baking sheet or platter and brush it with more of the syrupy aspic; chill until set. After the aspic has set, place the lobster carcass on the platter so that its claws surround the salad.

11. Referring to the photograph, one at a time, dip enough of the remaining 1 cup of peas and the rounds of pimiento into the remaining syrupy aspic and arrange them as shown, or as desired. Chill until the aspic has set. Finally, if desired, coat the vegetables, medallions, and lobster shell with more aspic and refrigerate until set. Serve cold.

5
Desserts

Beige-and-Brown Three-Tiered Cake

Unless you have an excellent bakery nearby, it's difficult to find an artfully decorated cake that tastes as good as it looks. Part of the reason for that is that most commercial bakers use white vegetable shortening instead of butter and confectioner's sugar in the frosting, which makes an overly sweet, fluffy concoction that only children seem to love.

Here's a recipe for making your own special "bakery-style" cake, suitable for the most important occasion. The only pan that you will need for it is a standard 13- by 9- by 2-inch cake pan. With this pan, you will bake two cakes, trim them into three rectangles, frost each with a distinctively rich coffee buttercream, and then stack them pyramid-style. Borders of mocha buttercream are then piped around the edges and the whole topped with quickly made chocolate leaves or a garland of fresh, real flowers.

Beige-and-Brown Three-Tiered Cake

Be sure that the tray you will be decorating this cake on fits into your refrigerator.
20 TO 24 SERVINGS

2 Vanilla Butter Cakes (recipe follows)
6 cups Coffee Buttercream Frosting (recipe follows), at room temperature

1½ cups Mocha Buttercream Frosting (see recipe for Coffee Buttercream Frosting, step 4)
about 30 Chocolate Leaves (instructions follow), in various sizes

1. Using a long, serrated knife, trim one cake to measure 7½ by 11¼ inches and place it on its serving tray. Cut the remaining cake into two rectangles—one that measures 5 by 8¾ inches, and the other, 2½ by 6½ inches. Place these last two rectangles of cake on a small baking sheet.

2. Using a spatula, spread a very thin layer of Coffee Buttercream Frosting over the sides and tops of all three layers to prevent crumbs from blending into the final frosting. Refrigerate all three layers until the buttercream has set and is chilled, about 1 hour. Cover all unused buttercream and keep at room temperature while the cakes are chilling.

3. Remove the tray containing the 7½- by 11¼-inch rectangle from the refrigerator and, using a spatula, frost it with ¼ inch of the buttercream. Return the cake to the refrigerator and remove the remaining two rectangles. Frost each of them with ¼ inch of the remaining buttercream. Chill all three rectangles until they have set, about 1 hour. If you are decorating with Chocolate Leaves, make them while the buttercream is setting.

4. Remove all three rectangles from the refrigerator. Run a knife under the medium-sized rectangle to loosen it from the baking sheet. With the help of a wide spatula or thin, stiff piece of cardboard, pick up the rectangle and center it over the 7½- by 11¼-inch rectangle. Then center the smallest rectangle on top (see illus. A).

ILLUSTRATION A

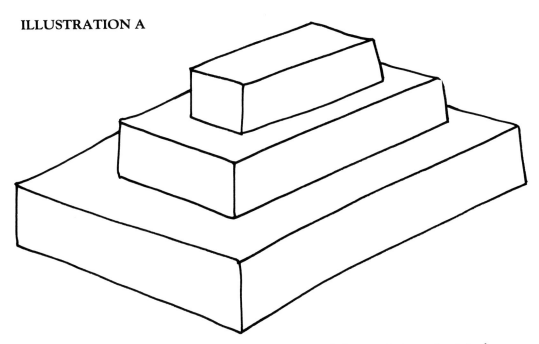

5. If you have any Coffee Buttercream Frosting left, stir it into the Mocha Frosting. You can add a little more cocoa to the Mocha Frosting if you wish, but since the color will become darker as the frosting sets, don't add much—the final color should be a medium shade. To pipe a shell border around the edges (see illus. B), fit a pastry bag with a star tip about ¼ inch wide (#18) and fill it

ILLUSTRATION B

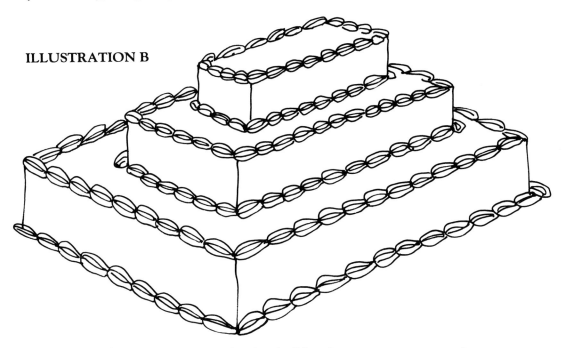

halfway with the frosting. To make the shell border (practice on waxed paper first and then scoop up the frosting before it sets and reuse it), hold the bag at a 45-degree angle with your right hand and use your left index finger to guide and steady the point as you move it. Squeeze out a shell shape, lifting the tip about ⅛ inch up from the surface and applying more pressure as you squeeze out the widest part of the shell; to taper off the shell, bring the point back down to the surface. Overlapping the point of the shell, squeeze out another shell (see illus. C-1 and C-2). Repeat the procedure all around the outside of each edge of the

ILLUSTRATION C-1

ILLUSTRATION C-2

cake. If desired, you can make a swirled shell border all around by simply pointing the widest part of the shells in opposite directions, first right, then left (see illus. C-3), or you might want to make a border of star shapes by simply

ILLUSTRATION C-3

squeezing the bag without lifting it up; when the size of star you desire has been squeezed out, lift the bag up and away.

6. If you are adding Chocolate Leaves, push them gently into the soft frosting in the desired places (see illus. D). Refrigerate the cake until about 1 hour (or up to 12 hours) before serving time, remove it from the refrigerator, and place it in a

ILLUSTRATION D

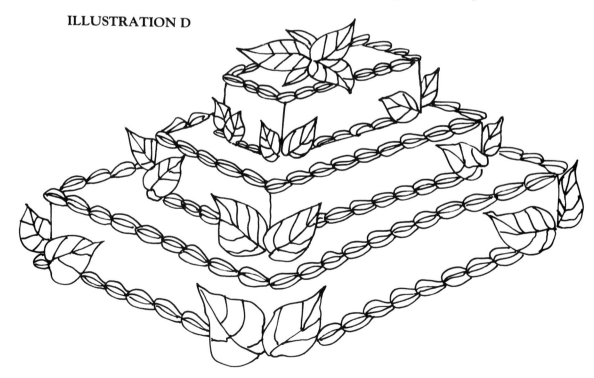

cool spot so that the butter in the buttercream won't melt but the chill will have been taken off the cake.

7. To serve, cut the top layer of the cake into two or three pieces and transfer them with a spatula to individual plates. Cut the middle layer into pieces and serve. Finally, cut the bottom layer into pieces and serve. Cover any uneaten cake and store in the refrigerator.

Vanilla Butter Cake

You will need to make two of these rich butter cakes to create this three-tiered cake. Mix one batch of batter and bake the cake before beginning the second one.

MAKES ONE CAKE, 7½ BY 11¼ INCHES (trimmed dimensions)

2⅔ cups all-purpose flour

2½ teaspoons baking powder

1 teaspoon salt

½ cup (1 stick) unsalted butter, at room temperature

1¾ cups sugar

1½ teaspoons vanilla extract

2 eggs

1¼ cups milk

1. Preheat the oven to 350°F. Lightly grease and flour a 13- by 9-inch baking pan, tapping out the excess flour.

2. In a medium-size bowl, combine the flour, baking powder, and salt; stir to blend and set aside. In a large mixing bowl, cream together the butter and sugar until light and fluffy. Add the vanilla and then beat in the eggs, one at a time, until well blended. Beat in one-third of the dry ingredients and then half of the milk. Repeat the procedure and then, finally, beat in the remaining third of the dry ingredients. Be sure to beat well after each addition.

3. Scrape the batter into the prepared pan. Spread the top so that it is level. Bake 35 to 45 minutes, or until the center of the top springs back when lightly touched (a toothpick will come out clean when inserted in the center and the edges of the cake will begin to pull away from the pan). Remove the cake from the oven and cool it in the pan set on a rack for 10 minutes. Invert the rack over the cake and then, holding the rack and the pan together, invert the cake onto the rack. Cool thoroughly.

4. Using exactly the same ingredients and procedures, make a second cake before beginning to assemble the tiered cake.

Coffee Buttercream Frosting

Some of this smooth buttercream is reserved for decoration (see step 4). After adding cocoa to the reserved portion, you will have Mocha Buttercream Frosting for decorating.
MAKES ABOUT 7½ CUPS (including 1½ cups Mocha Buttercream Frosting)

2 egg yolks
2 cups cold milk
⅓ cup cornstarch
5 cups sifted confectioner's sugar
3 tablespoons instant espresso coffee

powder
2½ cups (5 sticks) unsalted butter, at room temperature
3 tablespoons cocoa

1. In a medium-size, heatproof bowl, whisk together the egg yolks, 1 cup of the milk, and the cornstarch until smooth; set aside.

2. In a heavy, medium-size saucepan, combine the remaining 1 cup of milk, 2 cups of the confectioner's sugar, and all the instant espresso coffee powder. Stir to blend and then place over moderate heat. Stirring frequently, heat until the mixture just begins to boil. Remove from the heat. Whisk the egg yolk-cornstarch mixture to blend and then slowly whisk in the hot milk mixture. Place the mixture in a clean saucepan and set it over moderate heat. Whisking constantly and reducing the heat slightly if necessary to prevent sticking, cook the mixture until it comes to a full boil and is very thick (this is the buttercream base). Remove from the heat and scrape the mixture into a medium-size heatproof bowl. Cover the surface with a sheet of plastic wrap or waxed paper and cool to room temperature.

3. Because the buttercream base is so stiff after cooling to room temperature, it is easiest to use a heavy-duty mixer or a sturdy hand-held mixer for this step. Cream the butter with the remaining 3 cups of confectioner's sugar until light and fluffy, about 5 minutes. Continue to beat as you add the buttercream base ¼ cup at a time, beating well after each addition. When all has been blended in, beat until smooth (the final blending can be done in a food processor). Cover and keep at room temperature until needed for frosting, up to 3 hours ahead of time. If you want to keep the frosting overnight, refrigerate it, covered, and then allow it to soften to room temperature and beat again before using.

4. To make the Mocha Frosting for decorating, remove 1½ cups of the frosting and place it in a bowl; blend in the cocoa. Cover and reserve until needed.

Chocolate Leaves

Even though chocolate leaves look complicated to make, they are very easy to prepare. Basically, you simply brush melted chocolate over the backs of non-toxic leaves. Lemon leaves work very well for this, but other leaves with pronounced veins will also give good results.

If you want to decorate the cake as illustration D suggests, you will need about thirty leaves, ranging in size from small to large. Place 8 ounces of semisweet chocolate in the top portion of a double-boiler over (not touching) simmering water. After the chocolate has melted, stir only until smooth.

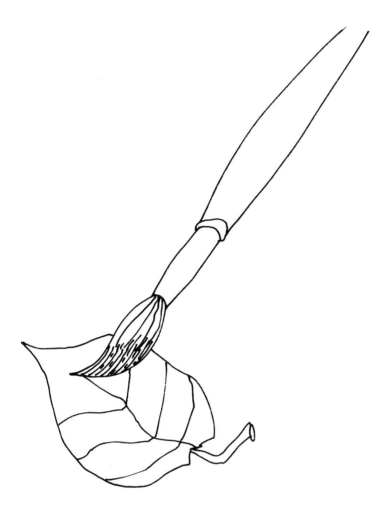

Remove the pan from the heat, but keep it over the hot water. Dip a pastry brush or a clean watercolor brush (#8) into the chocolate and paint a thin layer over the back of each leaf. When the chocolate begins to set, apply one more coat of chocolate, making the edge of the chocolate even with the edge of the leaf. Then refrigerate the leaves until set, about 10 minutes. Remove them from the refrigerator, and beginning at the stem end, carefully fold back and peel the real leaves away. Chill until needed.

Peach Melba Ice-Cream Bombe

A bombe is prepared simply by shaping slightly softened ice cream into concentric layers in a bombe mold or stainless-steel bowl, freezing it each time that you add a layer of flavor. This one combines the traditional melba ingredients of peaches and raspberries fortified with rum and brandy. When the bombe is frozen and cut into, the layers of ice cream reveal a center of rosy red raspberry sherbet. The mouth-watering combination of peaches, vanilla, and raspberries is further enhanced by the addition of a topping of ruby red Raspberry Sauce.

The bombe is easy to make, but it should be prepared and frozen the day before you plan to serve it.

Peach Melba Ice-Cream Bombe

Unless you feel like making your own ice cream, the ingredients for this recipe are simply a supermarket's shelf away. You will need a 3-quart bombe mold or a stainless-steel bowl.

12 TO 16 SERVINGS

1½ quarts vanilla ice cream, softened slightly	1 pint raspberry sherbet
1 teaspoon vanilla extract	3 tablespoons raspberry brandy or crème de cassis liqueur
¼ cup brandy	peach slices dipped in lemon juice
1 quart peach ice cream	or fresh raspberries for garnish
¼ cup dark rum	Raspberry Sauce (recipe follows)

1. In a large bowl, mix the vanilla ice cream with the vanilla and brandy until smooth. Transfer the ice cream to a 3-quart bombe mold or bowl. Freeze for 10 to 15 minutes, or until the ice cream is of a firm spreading consistency. Evenly spread the ice cream over the bottom and up the sides of the mold. Freeze until solid, about 2 hours, depending on your freezer. Near the completion of the freezing, remove the peach ice cream from the freezer and let it soften to a consistency that can be stirred, about 20 minutes, depending on how hard it is.

2. Place the softened peach ice cream in a medium-size bowl and stir in the rum until the mixture is smooth. Remove the mold containing the vanilla ice cream from the freezer and add the peach ice cream; return the mold to the freezer for 10 to 15 minutes, or until the ice cream is of a firm spreading consistency. Remove the mold from the freezer and spread the peach ice cream evenly over the vanilla ice cream. Freeze until solid, about 2 hours, depending on your freezer. Near the completion of the freezing, remove the raspberry sherbet from the freezer and let it soften to a consistency that can be mixed, about 15 minutes, depending on how hard it is.

3. Place the softened raspberry sherbet in a medium-size bowl and stir in the raspberry brandy until the mixture is smooth. Remove the mold from the freezer and pour the raspberry sherbet into the center of it to fill it. Cover the mold and freeze until solid, preferably overnight.

4. To unmold, dip the mold into hot water for about 5 seconds and invert it in the center of a serving plate. Lift the mold off the bombe. Garnish the edge all around with the peach slices that have been dipped in lemon juice or the raspberries. Using a long, sharp knife dipped in hot water, cut the bombe into wedges. Serve each slice with a spoonful of Raspberry Sauce.

Raspberry Sauce

This fragrant berry sauce can be made in a matter of minutes. Luckily, raspberries freeze well, so that you can make use of their fine flavor any time of the year.
MAKES ABOUT 1½ CUPS

  *2 packages (10 ounces each) quick-
    thaw frozen raspberries in syrup*

Thaw the raspberries. Place a wire strainer over a bowl. Add the berries and syrup to the strainer and push the mixture through the sieve, using a whisk or a spoon, to make a sauce. Discard the seeds left behind in the strainer.

Summer Fruit Tart

Here, fresh summer fruit easily becomes the colorful topping for a tempting fruit tart. You begin with a crisp butter-pastry shell and fill it to the brim with luscious Orange Cream. After the tart has been thoroughly chilled in the refrigerator to set the cream, peaches are sliced and arranged over it in an overlapping design. Borders of blueberries add a contrast in color as well as in flavor. Finally, a shimmering Apricot Glaze is brushed over the top to complete the tart. Instead of peaches, you can substitute unpeeled nectarines or apricots, and for the blueberries, strawberries, blackberries, or raspberries.

Summer Fruit Tart

The tart shell for this recipe can be baked, loosely covered, and kept at room temperature for as long as a day before you want to fill and serve it, but the fruit design should be applied shortly before serving. You will need an 11-inch tart pan with a removable bottom to make this recipe.
MAKES ONE 11-INCH TART

  *½ recipe Butter Pastry for Tart Shells
    (see recipe, p. 24, and step 1
    below)*
  *1¾ cups Orange Cream (recipe
    follows)*

  *3 medium-size to large, ripe,
    freestone peaches (1¼ pounds)*
  *1 cup blueberries, rinsed and picked
    over*
  ½ cup apricot preserves or jam

1. Prepare the Butter Pastry through step 2, using only 2 tablespoons of shortening. Pat the dough into a 6-inch round, wrap it tightly, and refrigerate for at least 2 hours or as long as overnight.

2. Preheat the oven to 400°F. On a lightly floured surface, roll the chilled pastry into a round 14 to 15 inches in diameter about ⅛ inch thick, working quickly to prevent the dough from becoming soft. Gently fold the round in half and then into quarters. Place the point of the triangle in the center of the bottom of an 11-inch tart pan and unfold, pressing the dough against the bottom and sides of the pan. Using a rolling pin, roll across the top of the tart pan to trim away the excess dough. With your fingers or the handle of a wooden spoon, press the dough into each groove of the tart pan. Line the pastry shell with aluminum foil, allowing 2 inches excess above the top of the pan. Carefully press the foil close to the dough and then fill the foil with pie weights, dried beans, or uncooked rice to prevent the dough from sagging. Bake for 10 to 12 minutes, or until the edge of the pastry has set all around and is just beginning to turn golden. Remove the aluminum-foil liner and the weights. Return the tart shell to the oven and, piercing the bottom with the tines of a fork if it starts to puff up, bake for an additional 10 to 12 minutes, or until golden brown. Place the pan on a rack and cool the shell to room temperature. Meanwhile, prepare the Orange Cream.

3. When the Orange Cream has cooled to room temperature, pour it into the baked tart shell, smooth the top, cover it with a round of waxed paper, and refrigerate until chilled, about 2 hours.

4. An hour or two before you plan to serve the tart, place about 2 quarts of water in a heavy, medium-size saucepan and bring it to a boil over high heat. Using a slotted spoon, lower one of the peaches into the water and blanch for 15 seconds from the time you place it into the water. Remove it with the slotted spoon and place it in a bowl of cold water. Repeat with the remaining two peaches. Using a paring knife, cut around the stem end of each and then carefully peel away the skin. Cut the peaches into quarters and then into vertical slices about ½ inch thick.

5. Remove the paper from the top of the Orange Cream. Referring to the illustration, edge the tart with a row of blueberries. Next, lay a row of peach

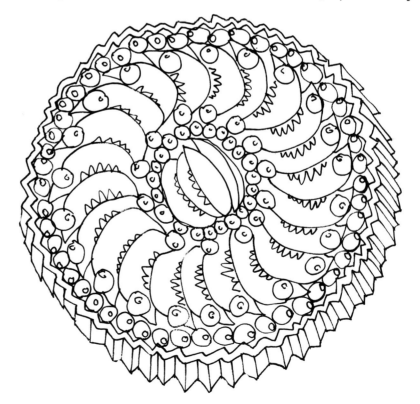

slices around the tart, slightly overlapping the ends that are nearest the center. Place five slices of peach in the center of the tart; the slice in the center should be placed skinned-side up and the two on either side should be overlapping on their sides. Decorate the center mound of peaches with a ring of blueberries. Place the remaining blueberries on top of the peach slices to complete both borders of berries.

6. Set a strainer over a small, heavy saucepan and push the apricot preserves or jam through with a spoon; scrape any that clings to the bottom of the strainer into the pan as well. Bring the preserves or jam to a boil and simmer for 3 minutes. Brush the glaze evenly over the fruit. Chill the tart until serving time and then cut it into wedges. Since this is a delicate tart, it is best to serve it within an hour or two after glazing.

Orange Cream

This cream should be cooled to room temperature before filling and chilling the prebaked tart shell.

MAKES ABOUT 1¾ CUPS

1¼ cups milk
3 egg yolks
⅓ cup sugar
⅓ cup all-purpose flour
3 tablespoons orange-flavored
   liqueur, such as Grand Marnier,

Cointreau, or Triple Sec, or fresh
   orange juice
2 teaspoons (packed) grated orange
   rind
4 tablespoons (½ stick) unsalted
   butter, sliced

1. Place the milk in a heavy, medium-size saucepan set over moderately low heat and, stirring frequently, bring the milk just to a boil; the surface will be foamy and rise about 1 inch (watch very carefully to prevent it from boiling over). Remove from the heat.

2. Meanwhile, place the egg yolks and sugar in a medium-size, heatproof bowl and whisk or beat the mixture for 1 or 2 minutes, or until light in color. Beat in the flour until smooth. Slowly add the hot milk, beating constantly.

3. Transfer the hot mixture to a clean, heavy saucepan and, stirring constantly, bring the mixture to a boil. (The mixture will be very thick.) Beat vigorously until it is smooth, and then boil gently, stirring constantly, for 3 minutes to cook the flour. Remove from the heat and stir in the liqueur or orange juice, grated rind, and the butter. When the butter has melted and the cream is smooth, cover it with a round of waxed paper and cool to room temperature.

Peach Parfait Cake

(Photograph on page 1)

Peaches and cream go together, well, like sugar and spice. Some marriages are meant to be. If you have a peach tree on your property, you might not realize just how lucky you are, for the peaches found in most markets have frequently been picked so early that they are hard and tasteless. When peaches are picked green, they never really ripen; the best you can do is to let them soften in a closed paper bag. Tree-ripened fruit is always the best. Pluck a peach from the tree and eat it as soon as possible.

When I was growing up on the West Coast, we had six varieties of peach trees. The first to bear ripened fruit offered small, sweet, fragrant white peaches so succulent that, when eaten, their juices would run down your chin. They were a positive hint of things to come during the months ahead, among which were the giant Elbertas, some larger than grapefruit. Although culinary experts never agree on which variety of peach has the best flavor and texture, I have always been very fond of those giant wonders of nature.

Since moving to Manhattan, the best I can do for peaches is to wait for summer when the farmer's market opens each Saturday morning. Over the years, I've given many of the farmers my recipes, and they, in turn, save the best of the crop for me. If the peaches are especially flavorful that day, I might buy a lug or two to make preserves and brandied peaches to savor for the winter, but I always save enough to eat unadorned, as nature intended, and some to slice and serve with sweet heavy cream. And, if I am having a small party at the peak of peach season, I will often use them to make this dramatic and delicious Peach Parfait Cake, which must be prepared the day of your party and kept chilled until you plan to serve it.

Peach Parfait Cake

Don't be alarmed that there is no baking powder or baking soda in this cake—it is a génoise cake, which means that it rises through the expansion of air bubbles trapped in the beaten eggs. After being baked, the cake is split into four layers and piled with whipped cream and peaches. You will need a 3-quart, stainless-steel bowl about 9 inches in diameter in which to bake the cake. Before beginning, make sure that you have enough space in the refrigerator to chill the cake.

MAKES ABOUT 20 SERVINGS

The Cake:
6 eggs, at room temperature
⅔ cup sugar
1½ teaspoons vanilla extract
1⅓ cups sifted all-purpose flour
  3 tablespoons unsalted butter, melted
    and cooled slightly

Filling and Decoration:
10 medium-size freestone peaches
  (about 4½ pounds)

¼ cup fresh lemon juice
5 cups heavy cream
1 teaspoon almond extract
1 cup sifted confectioner's sugar

Glaze:
1 jar (12 ounces) peach preserves
3 tablespoons brandy

1. Preheat the oven to 350°F. Lightly butter a 3-quart stainless-steel bowl approximately 9 inches in diameter. Dust the bowl lightly with flour and tap out the excess. Set the bowl aside. Chill another large bowl and beaters for whipping the cream in step 6.

2. Prepare the cake: A standard double-boiler will not work for this step, so you must create that effect by using a large stainless-steel or other heatproof bowl that will fit snugly into a deep saucepan yet have space below it for water. A bowl with a rim that rests on the edge on the pan is ideal, although if your bowl fits only halfway or three-fourths of the way into the pan, it will still work. Place enough water in the pan to come ½ to 1 inch below the bowl. Remove the bowl and bring the water to a simmer over moderate heat; reduce the heat slightly to maintain a simmer. Place the eggs in the bowl and whisk or beat them with a hand-held electric mixer on low speed only until blended. Place the bowl over the water, add the sugar, and, beating or whisking constantly, beat until the sugar has dissolved and the mixture is just warm to the touch. (Since timing may vary with the bowl that you are using, the only accurate way of testing for warmth is to dip your finger into the mixture.) Remove the bowl from the heat.

3. Vigorously whisk or beat the mixture with an electric mixer set at high speed until it has tripled in volume, 3 to 5 minutes. The mixture should be cool, light in color, and run off in a ribbon when the whisk is lifted. Stir in the vanilla.

4. A third at a time, sift the flour over the egg mixture, quickly folding it in with a rubber spatula. Fold in the melted butter and quickly but gently pour the batter into the prepared bowl. Bake the cake in the center of the oven for 45 to 50 minutes, or until the top springs back when lightly touched. Cool for 5 minutes. Then place a rack over the bowl and invert both, unmolding the cake onto the rack; cool thoroughly.

5. Prepare the filling: Peel the peaches (to facilitate peeling, place about three peaches at a time into boiling water for 15 to 30 seconds, rinse in cold water, and then, using a paring knife, peel the skin away from the pulp, beginning at the pointed end), cut them in half lengthwise, and remove the pits. Then cut the peach halves into slices about ½ inch thick and place them in a bowl with the lemon juice, tossing them so that all the slices are coated; set aside.

6. Using the chilled bowl and beaters from step 1 and working in two batches, whip half the heavy cream until soft peaks form. Add ½ teaspoon of the almond extract and ½ cup of the confectioner's sugar; beat until the cream is very stiff. Transfer it to another bowl, cover, and refrigerate until needed. Repeat with the remaining cream, almond extract, and confectioner's sugar.

7. Prepare the glaze: Place the preserves in a small saucepan and bring to a boil over moderate heat. Remove from the heat, stir in the brandy, and, with the back of a spoon, force all the preserves through a wire strainer placed over a bowl. Return the mixture to the pan and set aside.

8. Assemble the cake: Using a long, serrated knife, split the cake horizontally into four equal layers, using toothpicks to mark the layers first if necessary. Place the bottom layer on a cake plate, cut side up, and brush it with one-third of the warm glaze (if the glaze cools while you are assembling the cake, reheat it gently over low heat). Spread about ¼ inch of the whipped cream over the glaze and arrange about 1½ cups of the peach slices over the cream (reserve 20 slices of peach for decoration later). Top with ¼ inch of whipped cream. Add the next layer of cake and brush it with half the remaining warm glaze; top it with about ¼ inch of whipped cream and then arrange about 1 cup of peach slices over the cream. Spread additional whipped cream over the peaches until they are covered by ¼ inch. Add the third layer of cake, brush it with the remaining glaze, spread about ¼ inch of whipped cream over the glaze, and arrange about 1 cup of the peach slices over the cream. Spread the slices with ¼ inch of the whipped cream. Top with the remaining cake layer.

9. Decorate the cake: Reserving about 2 cups of the whipped cream for piping designs, use a spatula to frost the cake evenly with the remaining whipped cream. Arrange eight of the reserved peach slices on top of the cake in a spoke design. Fit a pastry bag with a ¼-inch star tip and fill it halfway with the reserved whipped cream. Pipe a shell design between each two peach slices on top of the cake (see the project photo and the instructions in step 5, p. 117, for decorating hints) and heart designs around the side of the cake. Evenly space ten or twelve of the reserved peach slices around the base of the cake and pipe a double swirl between each two. Chill the cake, uncovered, until serving time, or as long as 6 hours. Serve cold.

10. To serve the cake: Using a long, serrated knife and beginning at the top center of the cake, cut wedges down through the top two layers only. Transfer them to plates with a spatula and then cut the remaining bottom two layers into wedges and serve.

Berries and Bavarian-Cream Roll

There's a sweet surprise in store for your guests once this rectangular *trompe-l'oeil* dessert has been sliced into. The prize inside is a round swirl of raspberry jelly roll surrounded by cool, fresh Lemon Bavarian Cream. To serve the "berried" treasure, coat each dessert plate with a thin layer of Raspberry Sauce and top with a slice of the Berries and Bavarian-Cream Roll.

Although the cooking procedures used to create this fine dessert are standard, there are quite a few steps involved, so be sure to allow enough time for the preparation and chilling stages. Since the loaf must be refrigerated overnight before unmolding it, you have the added bonus of not having to worry about it the day of your dinner party.

Berries and Bavarian-Cream Roll

You will need a heavy jelly-roll pan that measures 18 by 13 inches and a 1-quart bread pan that measures 8 by 4 by 2½ inches to make this recipe.

8 SERVINGS

4 *eggs, separated and at room temperature (see Note)*	*pinch of salt*
½ *cup sugar*	2 *tablespoons confectioner's sugar*
1 *teaspoon vanilla extract*	⅓ *cup raspberry jam or preserves*
½ *cup plus 1 tablespoon all-purpose flour*	2½ *cups Lemon Bavarian Cream (recipe follows)*
2 *tablespoons melted unsalted butter, cooled slightly*	*thin lemon slices for garnish*
	¾ *cup Raspberry Sauce (see recipe, p. 123)*

Note: It is always easiest to separate eggs while cold and then let them come to room temperature, covered, in separate bowls.

1. Adjust an oven rack to the center of the oven and then preheat the oven to 400°F. Lightly butter a heavy 18- by 13-inch jelly-roll pan and then line it with waxed paper or parchment, allowing a 1-inch overhang at each end. Generously butter the paper and set the pan aside.

2. Prepare the cake: In a medium-size mixing bowl, combine the egg yolks and ¼ cup of the sugar. Beat with an electric mixer set at medium speed until light in color, 2 to 3 minutes. Blend in the vanilla, flour, and melted butter until smooth. Cover the bowl and set it aside.

3. Make the meringue: Wash and dry the beaters. Make sure that there is no egg yolk in the egg whites, or they will not fluff up properly (to remove a speck of yolk from the white, blot it with a small piece of bread). Put the egg whites in a medium-size mixing bowl, add the pinch of salt, and beat at high speed until greatly increased in volume and soft peaks form, 1 to 2 minutes. Begin to add the remaining ¼ cup sugar a tablespoon at a time, beating at medium speed until each spoonful is incorporated before adding the next. When all the sugar has been added, increase the speed to high and beat just until stiff peaks form; do not overbeat or the whites will become dry.

4. Working quickly but gently, fold about one-third of the meringue into the egg-yolk mixture. Using a spatula, scrape the egg-yolk mixture into the bowl of remaining meringue and gently fold it in until the color is even. (You must work rapidly to prevent the egg whites from losing their trapped air bubbles, which make the cake rise.)

5. Bake the cake: Quickly spread the batter as evenly as possible into the prepared pan and put it into the oven. Do not open the oven door for 5 minutes. The cake should be done in 5 to 7 minutes—the center will spring back when lightly touched and the edges will begin to brown slightly and pull away from the pan. While the cake is baking, place a sheet of waxed paper on your work surface and sift the confectioner's sugar evenly over it.

6. Remove the cake from the oven when it is done. If necessary, run the point of a knife around the edge of the pan to loosen the cake. Invert the cake onto the waxed paper. Using a pastry brush or clean sponge dampened with water, moisten the waxed paper attached to the cake; let it rest for 1 minute and then peel it off and discard. Let the cake cool to room temperature.

7. Lightly butter a 1-quart bread pan that measures 8 by 4 by 2½ inches. Referring to illustration A, line the pan with two strips of waxed paper, placing

ILLUSTRATION A

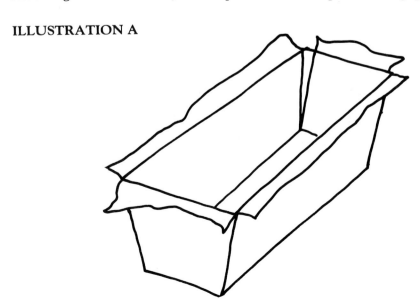

one lengthwise over the bottom and up the ends and the other crosswise over the bottom and up the sides. Lightly butter the waxed paper.

8. Make the jelly roll: If the edges of the cake are dry, trim away ⅛ to ¼ inch all around. Using a sharp knife, cut out a rectangle from one end that measures 8 by 10 inches (see illus. B), cutting through the waxed paper as you work. Place the

ILLUSTRATION B

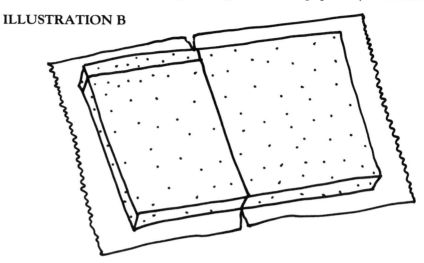

raspberry jam in a small bowl and break up any large pieces of berry with a fork. With a spatula or the back of a spoon, spread the jam evenly over the rectangle. Beginning with the 8-inch end closest to you, firmly roll up the cake to enclose the jam, peeling off the waxed paper as you roll (see illus. C). Wrap the jelly roll in more waxed paper and place it, seam-side down, on a plate in the refrigerator until needed.

ILLUSTRATION C

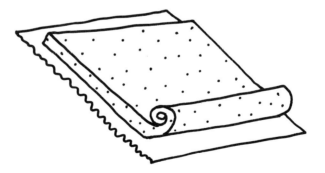

9. Line the loaf pan with cake: Turn the bread pan on one short end and trace around it on waxed paper or typing paper; cut out the shape to make a pattern. Place the pattern on one end of the remaining piece of cake and cut around it with a sharp knife; repeat to cut a second one (see illus. D). Place one piece of

ILLUSTRATION D

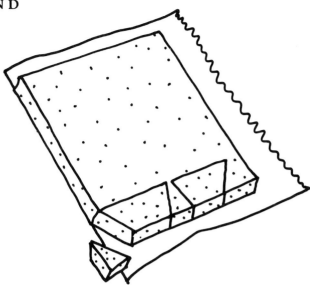

cake at each end of the pan, positioning the side that was face-down on your work surface against the paper in the pan (see illus. E). Cut the remaining sheet

ILLUSTRATION E

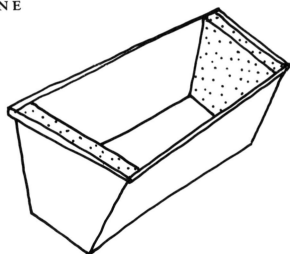

of cake into a rectangle that measures 7 by 8¼ inches. Trimming the rectangle slightly if necessary, fit the cake over the bottom of the pan and bring it up along the two long sides (see illus. F); there will be a small gap in each corner. If

ILLUSTRATION F

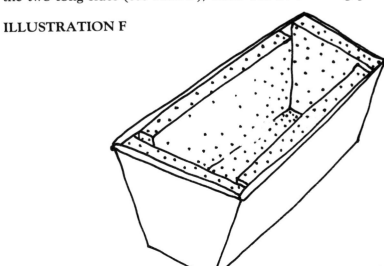

necessary, trim the top edges of the cake all around so that they are flush with the top of the pan. Cover and refrigerate until needed. Prepare the Lemon Bavarian Cream while the cake and jelly roll are chilling and cool it until it has the consistency of a thick, smooth syrup.

10. Final assembly: Pour ¾ cup of the syrupy Bavarian cream into the cake-lined pan and refrigerate or place in the freezer until the gelatin has just set. Keep the remaining Bavarian cream at room temperature to prevent its setting before you need to use it. If it should set, reheat it gently in a bowl of hot water until melted and then rechill it to the consistency of thick, smooth syrup.

11. When the first layer of Bavarian cream has set, trim both ends of the jelly roll so that it will fit, lengthwise, into the pan on top of the Bavarian cream. Center it on top of the Bavarian cream and pour enough additional Bavarian cream over the roll to reach halfway up the jelly roll. Refrigerate or freeze until it has just set. Fill the pan to the top with the remaining Bavarian cream, cover, and refrigerate for at least 12 hours or overnight.

ILLUSTRATION G

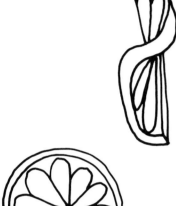

12. Prepare the garnish: Referring to illustration G, cut a slit halfway through each of three lemon slices, working from the center outward through the peel; twist the openings in opposite directions. Prepare the Raspberry Sauce, cover, and chill until serving time.

13. Unmold the dessert: Fill a pan or bowl with very hot water. Place the pan containing the Berries and Bavarian-Cream Roll into it for about 10 seconds. Remove, invert a flat serving plate over the pan, and then invert the dessert onto it. If it sticks, repeat the hot-water dipping process. Peel off the waxed paper and

ILLUSTRATION H

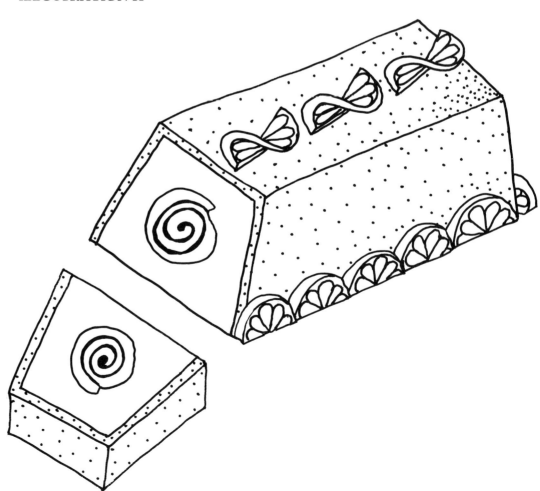

garnish the top with a row of the three lemon swirls (see illus. H). Cut more lemon slices in half crosswise and place all around the bottom of the dessert. Let the dessert rest at room temperature 15 minutes before serving.

14. Serve the dessert: Spoon about 1½ tablespoons of Raspberry Sauce onto each of eight dessert plates, tilting each plate so that the sauce coats evenly. Cut the dessert into eight slices and place one over the sauce on each plate.

Lemon Bavarian Cream
MAKES 2½ CUPS

2 cups milk
5 egg yolks
⅔ cup sugar
¼ cup fresh lemon juice

1 envelope (¼ ounce) plus 1 teaspoon unflavored gelatin
1 teaspoon (packed) grated lemon rind

1. Place the milk in a heavy, medium-size saucepan set over moderate heat and, stirring constantly, bring the milk just to the boiling point; the surface will be foamy and rise about 1 inch (watch carefully to prevent the milk from boiling over). Remove from the heat.

2. Place the egg yolks and sugar in a medium-size, heatproof bowl and beat or whisk them until light in color, 1 to 2 minutes. Slowly add the hot milk as you continue to beat until smooth. Transfer the hot mixture to a clean pan and place it over low heat. Stirring constantly, cook it until it thickens slightly and just coats a spoon (175°F.). Do not simmer or it will curdle. Immediately transfer the mixture to a bowl placed in another bowl filled with cold water and, stirring occasionally, cool the custard. (If it should curdle before you have a chance to transfer it to the bowl, add up to 2 tablespoons cold water, a drop at a time, whisking constantly. Then whisk in another egg yolk to bind the mixture and reheat it gently to thicken it slightly—the gelatin will later solidify it.)

3. Place the lemon juice, gelatin, and 1 tablespoon of cold water in a small, heatproof bowl or cup; stir to dissolve. Bring a small pan of water to a boil, remove it from the heat, place the bowl in it, and stir until the gelatin has melted. Pour the gelatin into the Bavarian cream and then stir in the lemon rind. Cool to room temperature. Stirring frequently, chill by setting the bowl in another bowl containing ice and water or by refrigerating until the mixture has the consistency of thick, smooth syrup. Then leave at room temperature.

6
Beverages

Liquados (Fresh Fruit Drinks)

(Photograph on p. 90)

In Mexico, *liquados* are sold in the marketplaces and on the streets just about everywhere one goes. Usually displayed in large glass barrels with wooden carrying handles, each one looks as refreshing as the next. The ice-cold beverages come in a rainbow of colors, and, for just a few pesos, they can quench your thirst on even the hottest of days. If you wish, add a jigger of rum to the *liquado* recipes here, top with a festive fruit garnish (instructions follow), relax in a hammock or under the shade of a tree, and pretend that you are south of the border.

Simple Syrup

Each of the drink recipes here requires a simple syrup. Make it ahead of time so that it will be at room temperature when you begin mixing the drinks. The recipe is easily cut in half if you wish to make fewer drinks.

MAKES 2 CUPS

2 cups sugar

Combine the sugar with 1 cup water in a medium-size saucepan. Stirring constantly, bring the mixture to a boil over moderate heat. Cool to room temperature.

Watermelon Cooler

MAKES 4½ CUPS

2 cups watermelon juice (see Note)	*½ cup Simple Syrup*
½ cup fresh lemon juice	*1½ cups seltzer water or club soda*

Note: A large watermelon can yield up to ½ gallon of juice, depending on its juiciness. There are three ways to extract the juice: Cut the melon into slices, remove the rind, and (1) use the bottom of a small bowl or cup to force the slices through a sieve into a bowl; (2) put it through a food mill fitted with a fine disk; or (3) remove the seeds and then put it through an electric juice extractor.

Combine the watermelon juice, lemon juice, and Simple Syrup in a pitcher and stir until thoroughly blended. Pour in the seltzer water or club soda, stir gently, and serve over ice. Add any of the following garnishes.

Pineapple Punch
MAKES 5 CUPS

2½ cups pineapple juice
½ cup Simple Syrup

2 cups seltzer water or club soda

Combine the pineapple juice and Simple Syrup in a pitcher; stir until thoroughly blended. Pour in the seltzer water or club soda, stir gently, and serve over ice. Add any of the following garnishes.

Orangeade
MAKES 5½ CUPS

2½ cups fresh orange juice
½ cup fresh lemon juice

½ cup Simple Syrup
2 cups seltzer water or club soda

Combine the orange juice, lemon juice, and Simple Syrup in a pitcher; stir until thoroughly blended. Pour in the seltzer water or club soda, stir gently, and serve over ice. Add any of the following garnishes.

Pink Lemonade
MAKES ABOUT 5¾ CUPS

1 cup fresh lemon juice
⅔ cup Simple Syrup

3 tablespoons grenadine syrup

Combine the lemon juice, Simple Syrup, grenadine syrup, and 4 cups water in a pitcher; stir until blended and pour over ice to serve. Add any of the following garnishes.

Limeade
MAKES 5⅔ CUPS

1 cup fresh lime juice

⅔ cup Simple Syrup

Combine the lime juice, Simple Syrup, and 4 cups water in a pitcher; stir until thoroughly blended. Serve over ice and add any of the following garnishes.

Fruit Garnishes

1. Referring to illustration A, cut a lemon, lime, or small orange slice that is slightly less than ¼ inch thick. Push a toothpick through the center and, if desired, push a cherry on the top end. Place a tall straw in the drink and insert the bottom of the toothpick into it.

ILLUSTRATION A

2. Referring to illustration B, cut a 1-inch cube of pineapple so that it tapers in slightly at the top. Insert a toothpick through the center and push a cherry on the top end. Place a straw in the drink and insert the bottom end of the toothpick into it.

ILLUSTRATION B

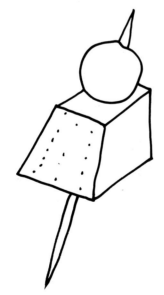

3. Referring to illustration C, cut a lemon, lime, or small orange slice that is about ¼ inch thick. Then carefully slice through only one half of it again (the top portion will still be one slice that is ¼ inch thick, while the bottom portion will be two slices, each ⅛ inch thick, but still attached to the thick portion). Insert the edge of the glass between the two bottom portions.

ILLUSTRATION C

ILLUSTRATION D

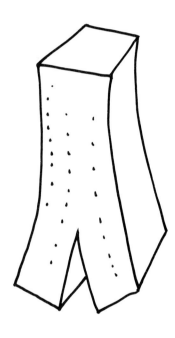

4. Referring to illustration D, trim a piece of fresh pineapple so that it measures ½ inch by 1 inch by 3 inches long. Cut a 1-inch-long slit into the center of the 1-inch width of the pineapple piece and insert the edge of a glass, spear the pineapple with a cherry-topped toothpick if desired, and garnish the drink with a sprig of mint.

5. Referring to illustration E, cut a lemon, lime, or small orange slice that is about ¼ inch thick. Insert a toothpick through the center of the rind, angle it so that it comes out of the center of the slice, and top it with a cherry. Insert the toothpick into a tall drinking straw and add to the drink.

ILLUSTRATION E

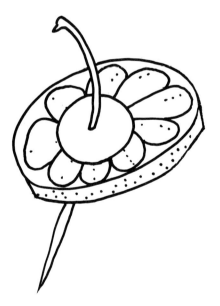

Festive Cocktails

There is nothing quite so colorful and welcome at a gathering as a well-made cocktail embellished with a simple garnish. It can cool one down on a scorching hot day or break the ice at a cocktail party.

The four drinks here were developed with the cocktail party in mind, but I confess that once in a while I make Margarita Spritzers just for myself at home.

Two of the drinks are garnished with fresh nontoxic flowers, one with a moon of orange rind, and the last, a simple but innovative double-cut slice of lime.

Margarita Spritzer

The classic Margarita can be too potent for many occasions, so I have devised this bubbly version lightened with club soda and garnished with a double-split lime. Since the proportion of the Margarita mixture to club soda is equal, you could easily increase the quantity and use it for a party punch bowl.

MAKES 3½ CUPS

½ cup fresh lime juice (reserve one or two of the rinds)

¾ cup orange-flavored liqueur, such as Triple Sec, Cointreau, or Grand Marnier

½ cup tequila

Margarita salt or coarse (kosher) salt (optional)

egg white (optional, see step 2)

1¾ cups club soda, chilled

Lime Garnishes (see step 3, p. 138)

1. In a small pitcher or cocktail shaker, combine the lime juice, orange-flavored liqueur, and tequila; stir to blend.

2. Place about ¼ cup of the optional salt on a small plate. Working with one old-fashioned glass at a time, first rub the rim with the moist side of a reserved lime rind and then invert it into the salt to lightly coat the edge. Repeat with additional glasses. If you are using this recipe as a punch, dip the rims of the glasses in lightly beaten egg white first before dipping them in salt and then let them dry for about an hour; the salt will hold in place.

3. Fill each glass with ice. Pour in about ⅓ cup of the Margarita mixture and then about ⅓ cup of the club soda; give it a stir, add the Lime Garnishes, and serve.

Orange Polar-Bear

When served in a stemmed cocktail glass, this frozen drink can be mounded and topped with a half ring of orange rind; if citrus trees happen to be in blossom, place a sprig at the edge of the glass.

MAKES ABOUT 2 CUPS

⅓ cup frozen orange-juice
   concentrate
⅓ cup vodka
3 tablespoons orange marmalade
2 tablespoons fresh lemon juice
1 tablespoon sugar, preferably
   superfine

½ teaspoon orange flower water
   (optional)
   pinch of ground cloves
8 to 10 ice cubes
   Orange-Rind Garnishes
   (instructions follow) or fresh citrus
   blossoms

In the container of a blender, combine the orange-juice concentrate, vodka, marmalade, lemon juice, sugar, optional orange flower water, and cloves; blend until smooth. Add eight of the ice cubes and blend at high speed until the mixture has the consistency of soft sherbet, about 2 minutes, adding one or two of the remaining ice cubes if necessary to achieve the desired consistency. Serve in stemmed cocktail glasses or old-fashioned glasses with the Orange-Rind Garnishes or sprigs of citrus blossoms.

Orange-Rind Garnishes

slices of orange, each ½ inch thick
whole cloves

Cut each slice in half and remove the flesh of the orange, leaving two half rings of rind from each slice. Insert cloves into the width of each rind on the outer surface (see illus. A). Use the garnish to top the Orange Polar-Bear.

ILLUSTRATION A

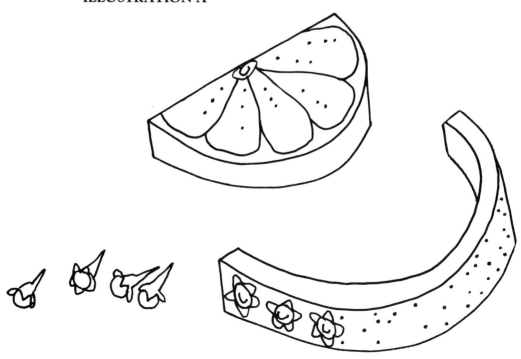

Martinique Cooler

This cooling fruit drink was inspired by a visit to the tropical paradise of Martinique. If you happen to be there or, for some other reason, have tropical flowers at hand, simply pluck one from a plant and use it to garnish the drinks. If the weather is very hot, you might like to add some club soda before serving this drink.

MAKES 3½ CUPS

1 cup fresh orange juice
1 cup pineapple juice
½ cup apricot nectar
2 tablespoons fresh lemon juice

2 tablespoons grenadine liqueur
¾ cup dark rum or to taste
fresh flower garnishes

1. In a small pitcher or a cocktail shaker, combine the orange juice, pineapple juice, apricot nectar, lemon juice, grenadine liqueur, and the rum; stir to blend.

2. Fill four tall, thin 12-ounce glasses to the top with ice cubes. Pour the juice-and-rum mixture over the ice and add a straw or two and a fresh flower garnish to complete the Martinique Cooler.

Apricot-Cream Fizz

Although delicious any time of the day, an Apricot-Cream Fizz is a soothing way to begin a brunch. This recipe will make enough to fill four 12-ounce stemmed glasses when filled with ice. The garnish, a fresh flower, can float on top if it's small or the stem of a sprig of flowers can be placed in the straw.

MAKES 3 CUPS

1 cup apricot nectar
½ cup vodka
¼ cup sour cream
2 tablespoons fresh lemon juice
2 tablespoons honey

¼ teaspoon almond extract
1 cup club soda, chilled
fresh flower garnishes

1. In the container of a blender, combine the apricot nectar, vodka, sour cream, lemon juice, honey, and almond extract; blend at high speed until smooth.

2. Fill four 12-ounce stemmed glasses with ice cubes. Pour ½ cup of the apricot mixture into each. Slowly pour ¼ cup of the club soda into each (the mixture will foam up to the top). Add a straw and a fresh flower garnish and serve.

Fruit Punches with Floating Garnishes

There are many advantages to serving a well-prepared punch at a party. At its best, it can be thirst-quenching, tasty, and less effort to serve than individual cocktails. A splendid garnish, floating in the center of the punch, can add an important festive touch. It can be as simple as a decorative "iceberg" embedded with fruit, orange slices studded with cloves, or, a little more involved, a sunburst fashioned from orange rind.

Orange Sunshine Punch

All the ingredients should be well chilled before mixing this recipe and the garnish prepared ahead of time.

MAKES ABOUT 5 QUARTS

1 *quart fresh orange juice*
1½ *cups peach nectar*
1 *cup brandy*
1½ *cups orange-flavored liqueur, such as Triple-Sec, Cointreau, or Grand Marnier*

2 *bottles (one fifth each) dry white wine*
2 *bottles (one fifth each) champagne Orange Sunshine Garnish (instructions follow)*

1. In a large punch bowl, place the orange juice, peach nectar, brandy, orange-flavored liqueur, and wine. Stir until blended.

2. Resting the neck of the champagne bottle on the side of the punch bowl, slowly pour it into the punch; repeat with the other bottle of champagne. Give the punch a gentle stir with a large spoon and then float the Orange Sunshine Garnish on top. Scatter some ice cubes around the garnish and serve cold.

Orange Sunshine Garnish

You can prepare this garnish, wrap it in damp paper towels, and keep it in the refrigerator for as long as six hours before you need it.

MAKES 1 GARNISH

You will need two medium-size oranges and one large one to make this decoration. If you wish, mark lines on the orange with a nontoxic wax crayon before you cut into it. Then, using a sharp paring knife, make zigzag cuts in the large orange so that it has twelve pointed sections (see illus. A). Each cut should be made all the way through the peel but not deeply into the orange; the points should almost reach the stem end and stop about 1 inch from the bottom of the orange. Discard the top portion of peel (the stem end) and then gently remove the sections of orange with your fingers (reserve them for another use). You will

ILLUSTRATION A

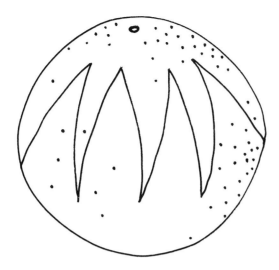

now have a hollow orange rind with twelve long points (see illus. B). If necessary, gently scrape the inside of the rind with a spoon to make it smooth. Repeat with the other two oranges.

ILLUSTRATION B

ILLUSTRATION C

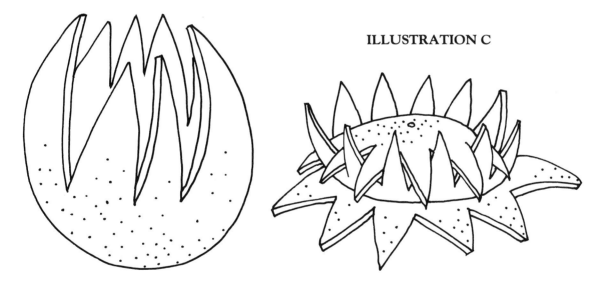

Referring to illustration C and starting with the largest orange, place it skin side up on your work surface. Gently push on it with your hands to flatten it as much as possible; then push on the center to make it slightly concave. Set one of the remaining orange peels, points up, on top of the concave portion and secure it from underneath with three toothpicks. Invert the third orange peel on top of the one you just secured, placing each point between two below it. Float the garnish in the punch immediately or wrap it in damp paper towels and refrigerate until needed.

St. Peter's Punch

You might want to serve this punch during the fall and winter when apples are at their best, but you need not restrict yourself seasonally because good apple juice is available all year long. The apple juice, bourbon, and club soda should be well chilled before beginning this recipe.

MAKES ABOUT 3 QUARTS

⅓ cup brown sugar
½ teaspoon cinnamon
¼ teaspoon ground cloves
2 quarts apple juice
2 cups bourbon
1 cup orange-flavored liqueur, such

as Triple Sec, Cointreau, or Grand Marnier
¼ cup fresh lemon juice
1 bottle (12 ounces) club soda
3 Clove-Studded Orange Slices (instructions follow)

1. Combine the brown sugar, cinnamon, and cloves in a small saucepan and stir to blend. Add 1 cup of the apple juice and place the pan over moderate heat. Stirring frequently, bring the mixture to a simmer; remove from the heat and stir until the brown sugar has dissolved. Set aside to cool to room temperature.

2. In a punch bowl, pour the remaining apple juice, the bourbon, orange-flavored liqueur, and lemon juice. Stir in the dissolved cinnamon sugar. Resting the neck of the bottle on the edge of the bowl, pour in the club soda. Give the punch a gentle stir and float the Clove-Studded Orange Slices on top. Surround the slices with ice cubes and serve cold.

Clove-Studded Orange Slices

Cut three slices, each ½ inch thick, from the center of a large orange. Insert cloves all around the width of the outer edge of each slice, as shown in the illustration.

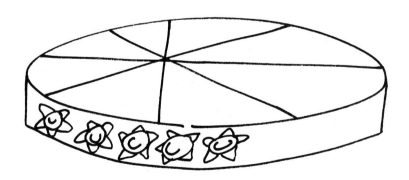

Champagne-and-Raspberry Punch

This seductively delicious punch has a garnish of raspberries frozen in ice; if you have mint leaves, you can add them to the garnish as well. For large gatherings, simply increase the ingredients of the punch proportionally.

MAKES ABOUT 2½ QUARTS

2 cups brandy
1 package (10 ounces) quick-thaw
   frozen raspberries in syrup, thawed
1 package (10 ounces) quick-thaw
   frozen peaches in syrup, thawed
¼ cup fresh lemon juice

1 bottle (one fifth) champagne or
   sparkling wine, chilled
1 bottle (12 ounces) club soda,
   chilled
   Frozen Raspberry Garnish
   (instructions follow)

1. Place 1 cup of the brandy in the container of a blender along with the raspberries and peaches and their syrups and purée. Pour the mixture through a strainer into a punch bowl, pushing it through with the back of a spoon; discard the solids left behind in the strainer. Stir in the remaining brandy and the lemon juice.

2. Resting the neck of the champagne or sparkling-wine bottle on the edge of the punch bowl, gently pour it into the punch; add the club soda in the same manner. Give the punch a gentle stir with a large spoon and float the Frozen Raspberry Garnish in the center. Serve cold.

Frozen Raspberry Garnish

Choose a shallow, heart-shaped (or other shape) mold that measures 6 to 8 inches across. Fill it with ½ inch of water and freeze it until solid. Arrange about eighteen whole raspberries (or other fruit) into clusters, adding some mint leaves if desired, over the ice. Add about ¼ inch of water (just enough to coat the ice without disturbing the design) and freeze until solid—this will hold the design in place. Fill the mold to the top with cold water and freeze until solid. If you plan to fill the punch bowl more than once, make enough Frozen Raspberry Garnishes so that you can add a fresh one each time you fill the bowl. They can be made a week before you need them and stored in the freezer.

Ice-Cream and Sherbet Freezes with Chocolate Silhouettes

Ice-cream freezes are very popular in some parts of this country, but they are absent from most soda-fountain menus in New York City. Perhaps many people don't know what they are. Quite simply, they are a combination of carbonated, flavored soda and ice cream blended to a thick, milk-shake consistency. When fanciful Chocolate Silhouettes on straws are added, you have a charming solution to the question of what beverage to serve at the children's party or any other special occasion. The Chocolate Silhouettes are easily made by pouring melted chocolate into shapes on aluminum foil and embedding straws into the chocolate before it sets. They can be made as long as two days ahead of time and then refrigerated until needed.

Vanilla Root-Beer Freeze
MAKES TWO 10-OUNCE SERVINGS

1 pint vanilla ice cream
¾ to 1 cup root beer, chilled

2 to 4 Chocolate Silhouettes
(instructions follow)

Let the ice cream soften at room temperature only until it can easily be scooped from the container. Then place it and ¾ cup of the root beer in the container of a blender. Blend just until smooth, adding the remaining root beer if the freeze is too thick. Pour into two 10-ounce soda-fountain glasses, garnish each with one or two Chocolate Silhouettes, and serve immediately.

Triple Chocolate Freeze
MAKES TWO 10-OUNCE SERVINGS

1 pint chocolate ice cream
¾ to 1 cup carbonated chocolate
soda, chilled

2 to 4 Chocolate Silhouettes
(instructions follow)

Let the ice cream soften at room temperature only until it can easily be scooped from the container. Place it and ¾ cup of the chocolate soda in the container of a blender. Blend just until smooth, adding the remaining soda if the freeze is too thick. Pour into two 10-ounce soda-fountain glasses, garnish each with one or two Chocolate Silhouettes, and serve immediately.

Raspberry-Ginger Freeze

MAKES TWO 10-OUNCE SERVINGS

1 pint raspberry sherbet
¾ to 1 cup gingerale, chilled

2 to 4 Chocolate Silhouettes
(instructions follow)

Let the sherbet soften at room temperature only until it can be easily scooped from the container. Place it and ¾ cup of the gingerale in the container of a blender. Blend just until smooth, adding the remaining gingerale if the freeze is too thick. Pour into two 10-ounce soda-fountain glasses, garnish each with one or two Chocolate Silhouettes, and serve immediately.

Chocolate Silhouettes

To make these chocolate whimsies, trace the patterns on page 54 onto squares of aluminum foil and then spoon melted chocolate into the shape. Finally, lay a straw or an ice-cream stick in the soft chocolate. After chilling, use the Chocolate Silhouettes to garnish the Ice-Cream and Sherbet Freezes.

MAKES ABOUT 12

3 squares (1 ounce each) semisweet
chocolate

straws or wooden ice-cream sticks

1. Trace around the shapes from page 54 (shaped biscuit patterns) on tracing paper and cut them out. Cut aluminum foil into 4-inch squares, lay a paper pattern on each, and, using a toothpick, trace around them.

2. Place the chocolate in the top portion of a double-boiler and set over simmering water. Stir occasionally until melted. Remove from the heat but leave the chocolate over hot water while you work.

3. Working on a baking sheet, use a small spoon to place some of the chocolate in the center of the shape on the foil. Use a toothpick to spread it out thinly over the shape and to form the edges. Press about ½ inch of the end of a straw or ice-cream stick into the bottom of the shape. Repeat with the remaining chocolate. Refrigerate for 10 to 15 minutes, or until the chocolate has set. Chocolate Silhouettes can be kept in the refrigerator for a day or two before using to garnish.

7
Holiday Recipes

Roast Leg of Pork
With Turnip Calla Lilies

Agood way to celebrate the arrival of spring is to invite some friends to a daytime Sunday dinner party. Have an abundant assortment of hors d'oeuvre on hand, some good wine, and a selection of music to entertain everyone until dinnertime. Restrict the dinner menu to dishes that will hold up well, such as the following roast leg of pork or a smoked ham, either of which can be served hot, warm, or cold. Create some beautiful white calla lilies ahead of time from thinly sliced turnips and baby carrots and trail them gracefully around the roast. Finally, for a perfect accompaniment, parboil a selection of spring vegetables, also ahead of time, and reheat them in melted butter at serving time.

Roast Leg of Pork with Turnip Calla Lilies

A leg of pork is frequently called a fresh ham, but since it is neither smoked nor cured, roast leg of pork is probably a more accurate title for this recipe. If you would prefer to serve a smoked ham for your spring celebration, do so, but garnish it with the beautiful, edible Turnip Calla Lilies you can make by following the instructions at the end of this recipe.

16 SERVINGS

12- to 16-pound fresh leg of pork or
  fresh ham with bone in
1 large garlic clove, sliced in half
  crosswise
2 teaspoons crumbled sage or thyme
  (or your favorite herb)

about 12 Turnip Calla Lilies
  with scallion or leek greens
  (instructions follow)

1. Preheat the oven to 450°F. Choose a roasting pan with a rack that is just slightly larger than the leg of pork. Using a sharp knife, score the skin of the leg in a ½-inch-wide diamond pattern, cutting through the skin and into the fat about ⅛ inch; do not cut into the meat. Rub the leg all over with the garlic and then the sage or thyme. Place the meat, scored-side up, on the rack, set the rack in the roasting pan, and place it in the oven. After 10 minutes, reduce the heat to 325°F. and roast, basting occasionally after the first hour, until the internal temperature reaches 165°F., about 25 minutes per pound. To check the temperature, insert a meat thermometer into the thickest part of the meat without touching the bone.

2. Increase the temperature to 450°F. and roast for about 15 minutes to make the skin crisp. Remove from the oven and let the roast rest for 20 minutes. Then place on a serving platter, garnish with the Turnip Calla Lilies and scallion or leek greens, and serve hot, warm, or cool.

Calla Lilies

ILLUSTRATION A

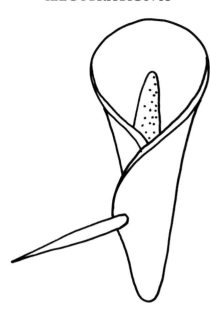

White or yellow turnips can be peeled and thinly sliced and then fashioned into lilies by wrapping the slices around baby carrots or trimmed carrot sticks. They will keep overnight if they have been placed in ice water and are then refrigerated. With the addition of scallion greens or leaves of leek, they make a beautiful garnish around a leg of pork or glazed ham for a special spring dinner.

To make about twelve lilies, you will need one 8-ounce turnip and twelve baby carrots, each about 3 inches long, or several regular-size carrots shaved with a vegetable peeler to a diameter slightly thicker than that of a pencil and then cut into 3-inch lengths. If you are using regular-size carrots, use the vegetable peeler to round one end of each carrot piece (see illus. A).

Cut the turnip crosswise into paper-thin slices ($\frac{1}{16}$ inch or less) with a very sharp knife or vegetable slicer. Referring to illustration A, wrap one slice around a length of carrot so that the point of the carrot is upward and the turnip slice overlaps near the base (rounded portion) of the carrot; hold it in place with a toothpick. Place the lily in ice water and continue to make as many as desired. When ready to garnish the platter, remove the lilies from the water and snip off most of the toothpick, using poultry shears or wire cutters. Arrange them around the ham, using scallion greens or the green portions of a leek cut into pointed shapes between and around the flowers (see illus. B).

ILLUSTRATION B

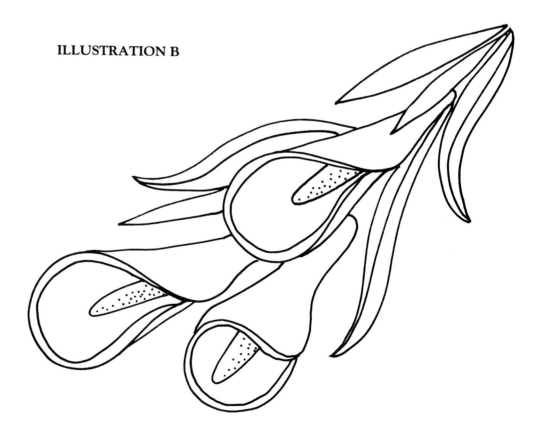

The Well-Dressed Turkey

(Photograph on page 93)

Even the stuffiest of Thanksgiving guests will applaud your holiday turkey when it, too, is "dressed for dinner." So this year, spiff up the All-American bird with a tailor-made pastry outfit.

This one wears a sensible suit of flaky butter pastry that includes a formal vest, button-down spats, and a bow tie all brushed with egg yolk and baked to golden perfection. For added elegance, a yellow rose was attached for a boutonniere. To complete the festivities, surround your Well-Dressed Turkey with Frosted Grapes and serve it with your favorite or traditional Thanksgiving accompaniments.

The Well-Dressed Turkey

For a large party, you might consider roasting one or two turkey breasts in addition to the whole turkey, to be sliced, arranged on a platter, and served, allowing the Well-Dressed Turkey to remain as the centerpiece until you wish to carve it. You can make the patterns for the pastry outfit (instructions follow), as well as the Butter Pastry, a day or two before you plan to use them.

18 SERVINGS

1 recipe Butter Pastry, chilled, using two egg yolks instead of one for glazing (see recipe, p. 24, and step 1 below)

1 turkey (18 pounds), thawed if frozen

½ cup (1 stick) unsalted butter, melted

Frosted Grapes for garnish (recipe follows)

1. Prepare the Butter Pastry: Follow the recipe for Butter Pastry through step 3, shaping the pastry into one flat round instead of two, wrapping it tightly, and chilling it for at least 2 hours or as long as two days before using. Prepare the following pastry-outfit patterns and set them aside until you will be cooking the turkey. Then, while the turkey is roasting, roll out the pastry, cut the shapes, and chill them until the turkey is done.

2. Prepare the turkey: Preheat the oven to 325°F. Remove the neck and giblets from the turkey and, if desired, reserve them for gravy or a stuffing recipe. If your turkey has a metal clamp holding the drumsticks together, remove and discard it. Rinse the turkey inside and out with cold running water and pat dry. Place the turkey, breast side down, on your work surface and fasten the neck skin to the back of the turkey with skewers or wooden picks. Turn the turkey breast side up, and tuck the wing tips under the bird. Using string, tie the drumsticks together.

3. Place the turkey, breast side up, on a rack in a roasting pan and brush it all over with some of the melted butter. Place it on a shelf set in the lower third of the oven and roast for 1 hour. Then baste it with more melted butter and some of the drippings. Continuing to baste every 30 minutes, roast the turkey for another 3½ to 4½ hours, or until done—the juices will run clear when the thickest part of the thigh is pierced with a fork or a meat thermometer inserted into the thickest part, without touching the bone, should read 175°F. If the skin becomes darker than a pale golden brown during roasting, tent the turkey loosely with aluminum foil and continue roasting. (The turkey will brown further during the additional time that the pastry outfit takes to bake.) Remove the turkey from the oven and increase the temperature to 400°F. Sever and discard the string holding the drumsticks together and let the turkey rest for 10 minutes.

4. Carefully place the vest over the breast of the turkey so that the small V-shape at the bottom of the vest is about 1 inch from the tip of the breast bone (see illus.

ILLUSTRATION A

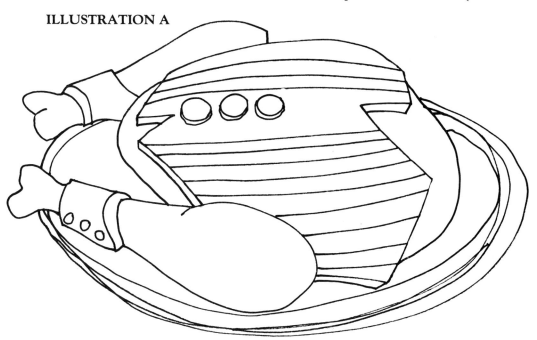

A) and gently press on the vest to make it conform to the shape of the turkey breast. Since the vest is large, another pair of hands or a floured spatula may be helpful in the transfer. Drape one spat over each drumstick so that the buttons face outward from the turkey (see illus. A). Paint the back of the bow tie with egg yolk and place it on the vest near the large V-shape; press on it gently so that it adheres. Return the turkey to the oven and bake only until the pastry is golden brown and crisp, 12 to 20 minutes (the time may vary greatly according to the type and size of your oven). If at any time the legs of the turkey begin to brown too quickly, cover them loosely with separate small sheets of aluminum foil. Remove the turkey from the oven, place it on a platter, garnish with the Frosted Green Grapes, and serve.

How to Make the Pastry Patterns

Materials Needed:
paper ruled with a 1-inch grid
brown wrapping paper
scissors

Working on the grid, enlarge the following pattern designs square by square, duplicating the lines in each square of the pattern in the corresponding square of the 1-inch grid. Enlarge all the pattern pieces, cut them out, and then trace around them on brown wrapping paper. Before you make the vest section of the pattern, fold a sheet of brown wrapping paper in half and lay the dotted line of the pattern along the fold; cut out the shape and unfold it—you will have the entire vest pattern. Cut out the remaining pieces from the brown wrapping paper and set aside.

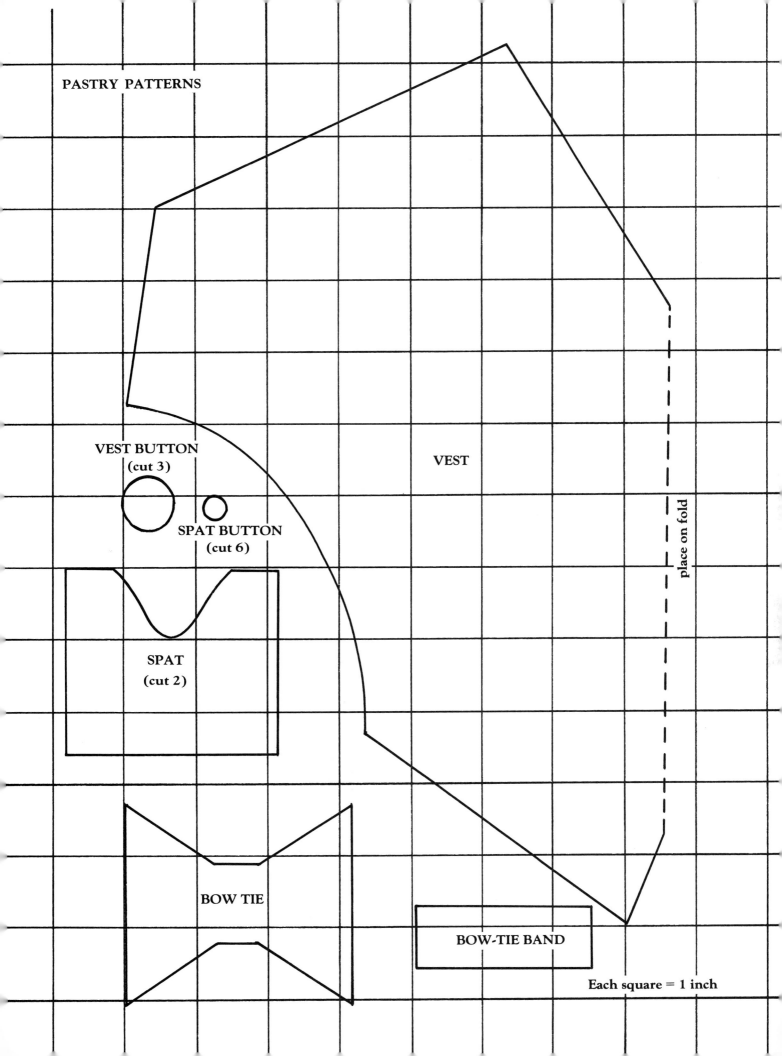

PASTRY PATTERNS

VEST

VEST BUTTON
(cut 3)

SPAT BUTTON
(cut 6)

SPAT
(cut 2)

place on fold

BOW TIE

BOW-TIE BAND

Each square = 1 inch

How to Make the Pastry Outfit

1. On a lightly floured surface with a floured rolling pin, roll the pastry out until it is slightly thicker than ⅛ inch.

2. Place the vest pattern on the pastry and cut around it with a paring knife. Do the same with the bow tie and bow-tie band and then cut out two spats. Using the vest-button pattern (or a small spice-jar cap), cut out three buttons. Using the spat-button pattern (or the small end of a funnel), cut out six spat buttons. Carefully gather all excess pieces of dough from around the pastry pieces, shape them into an oval about 5 inches long by 2 inches wide, wrap them tightly, and refrigerate until chilled.

3. Using a floured spatula along with your hands, carefully transfer the vest piece to a lightly floured cookie sheet. Using a floured spatula, transfer the remaining pieces to the cookie sheet. Cover with waxed paper and chill until needed.

4. When the excess dough has chilled, roll it out on a lightly floured surface to a rectangle that is slightly thicker than ⅛ inch and measures about 5 by 12 inches. To make the stripes for the vest, use a pastry wheel with a crimped edge or a ruler and paring knife to cut six strips that are ½ inch wide by 11 inches long and four strips that are ½ inch wide by 5 inches long. Place the strips on a lightly floured cookie sheet, cover with waxed paper, and refrigerate until chilled.

5. In a small bowl, lightly beat the 2 egg yolks with 1 tablespoon of water. Remove the baking sheet containing the pastry vest from the refrigerator. Brush the backs of the three vest buttons with egg yolk and attach them to the lower portion of the vest, making sure that they are centered in a straight line (see illus. A). Press gently to adhere them to the vest. Remove the chilled pastry strips from the refrigerator. Working outward from the center with one strip at a time and using the six long strips first, paint the backs with egg yolk and attach them evenly spaced in two rows of three near the vest buttons (see illus. B). Gently press them in place and trim the ends to conform to the vest shape. Continue with the remaining shorter strips, trimming as necessary. Attach the spat buttons to the spats in the same manner (see illus. C). Paint one side of the bow-tie band with egg yolk and wrap it, painted side down, around the center of the bow tie (see illus. D), pressing the band so that it adheres. As each piece is completed, leave it on the baking sheet. (If you overhandle the dough, the butter in it will become soft; if this happens, refrigerate the dough until firm before proceeding.) Using the egg-yolk mixture as a glaze, paint the stripes on the vest, the buttons on the spats, and the vest and the band on the bow tie. Refrigerate until the dough is firm and the egg yolk has dried. Paint the entire surface of the vest, bow tie, and spats with more egg yolk. Refrigerate until the turkey is fully cooked.

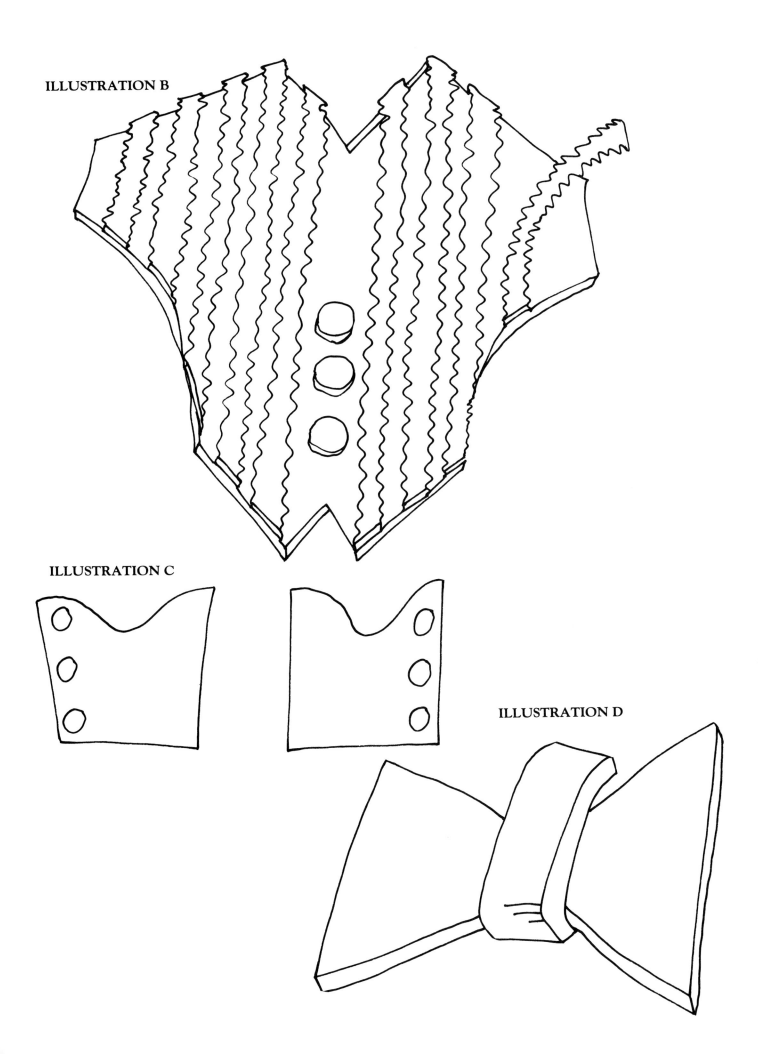

ILLUSTRATION B

ILLUSTRATION C

ILLUSTRATION D

Frosted Grapes

Prepare these grapes several hours ahead of time to allow them time to air-dry before using them as a garnish around your turkey platter.

2 pounds seedless green grapes, washed and dried
2 egg whites
1 cup sugar

1. Cut the grapes into small clusters. Place the egg whites in a medium-size mixing bowl and beat with a whisk or electric mixer until frothy. Place the sugar in a shallow bowl.

2. Dip each cluster of grapes into the egg white and then roll in the sugar, sprinkling more sugar over them as needed until they are just coated. Place the clusters on a rack and let them dry at room temperature for about 3 hours. Use them to garnish the holiday turkey platter.

Upside-Down Apple Pie

Who says that an apple pie must always look traditional? Not me—I'm willing to try anything when it comes to food. Sometimes the inspiration for a new food concept or recipe comes to me in a dream; at other times it strikes my head like a bolt of lightning. I was working at perfecting various upside-down cakes when I first thought about upside-down pies. Why not? They can certainly be turned out of the pan if the crust is even all around. After considerable experimentation, the classic American apple pie produced the best upside-down results.

Once you have flipped the pie over, you quickly spread the crust with Brown Sugar Glaze and decorate it with pecans or walnuts. Before serving, add some freshly whipped cream and red and green glacéed cherries. If you want to gild the lily, serve the pie, warm, with a scoop of homemade vanilla ice cream.

Upside-Down Apple Pie

The pastry for this recipe can be prepared the day before you make the pie.
MAKES ONE 9-INCH PIE

Flaky Pastry (recipe follows)
2½ pounds (about 7 medium-size) tart green cooking apples, such as Granny Smith
¾ cup sugar
3 tablespoons all-purpose flour
1 teaspoon cinnamon

3 tablespoons unsalted butter, cut into bits
Brown Sugar Glaze (recipe follows)
walnut or pecan halves
Whipped Cream (recipe follows)
1 red and 1 green glacéed cherry

1. Prepare the pastry: Lightly grease a 9-inch pie pan with vegetable shortening. Lightly flour a work surface and a rolling pin. Roll out half the dough to a ⅛-inch thickness and line the pie pan with it, taking care not to stretch the dough. Trim the dough so that there is a ½-inch overhang all around. Cover it and refrigerate until ready to assemble the pie. Roll out the second piece of dough to a ⅛-inch thickness, place it on a lightly floured cookie sheet, cover it, and chill until needed.

2. Prepare the apple filling: Preheat the oven to 425°F. Peel and core five of the apples and cut them into ¼-inch-thick slices. Measure the slices; you should have about 7 cups (packed). If you have less, slice as many of the remaining apples as necessary. Place the slices in a large bowl. In a small bowl, combine the sugar, flour, and cinnamon. Sprinkle the sugar mixture over the apples and toss until the apples are evenly coated.

3. Assemble the pie: Remove the prepared pie pan from the refrigerator. Neatly arrange the apple slices in the pie pan, beginning around the outer edge and working toward the center. Continue layering (packing them together) until you have used all the apples; pour any liquid remaining in the bowl over them. (The apples will be higher than the edge of the pie pan, but they will shrink during baking.) Dot the apples with the bits of butter. With a pastry brush or your fingers, generously moisten the ½-inch overhang of pastry all around. Remove the dough on the cookie sheet from the refrigerator; cut three small holes for steam vents in the center and carefully slide the dough in place over the apples. Trim the top dough so that it has a ½ inch overhang, and pinch the two overhanging pieces of pastry together. Then fold half the overhang under all around so that the edge of the pastry is even with the pie pan.

4. Bake the pie: Place the pie on a baking sheet, set on a rack in the lower third of the oven, and bake for 50 to 60 minutes, or until a toothpick inserted through one of the steam vents into an apple easily pierces it. Remove the pie from the oven and cool for 10 minutes. Invert a serving plate over the pie (to force the raised portion flush with the top edge of the pie pan) and, holding both together firmly with potholders, invert so that the pie unmolds, upside down, onto the plate.

5. To assemble, immediately prepare the Brown Sugar Glaze and pour over the crust, using the back of a spoon to spread it rapidly in a circular motion from the center out to the edge of the pie. Quickly arrange the walnut or pecan halves evenly around the edge and then allow the pie to reach room temperature. Before serving, fit a pastry bag with a ¼-inch star tip and fill with about half the Whipped Cream. Pipe stars all around the edge of the pie and then pipe a larger rosette in the center. Top the rosette with a red glacéed cherry and a slice of green glacéed cherry on either side of it. Serve the pie with the remaining Whipped Cream or vanilla ice cream.

Flaky Pastry
MAKES ENOUGH FOR ONE 9-INCH DOUBLE-CRUST PIE

2 cups all-purpose flour
¼ teaspoon salt
1 teaspoon sugar

⅔ cup vegetable shortening
about ¼ cup ice water

In a large mixing bowl, combine the flour, salt, and sugar. Cut in the shortening with a pastry blender or two knives until the mixture resembles coarse meal. Sprinkle the ice water over the flour mixture and stir quickly with a fork just until the dough can be gathered into a ball. (It may be necessary to add a few more drops of ice water, but avoid overworking the dough or letting it become warm; if you do, it will be tough when baked.) Divide the dough in half, wrap each separately, and chill for at least 1 hour or as long as a day before using.

Brown Sugar Glaze

This glaze should be made and poured over the pie as soon as the pie has been unmolded because it sets very quickly.

MAKES ENOUGH TO GLAZE ONE 9-INCH PIE

¼ cup (packed) dark brown sugar
2 tablespoons milk
1 cup sifted confectioner's sugar

In a small, heavy saucepan, combine the brown sugar and milk. Bring the mixture to a boil over moderate heat, stirring constantly. Remove from the heat and stir in the confectioner's sugar.

Whipped Cream

MAKES 2 CUPS

1 cup heavy cream, chilled
½ cup sifted confectioner's sugar

Chill a whisk or the beaters to an electric mixer and a medium-size bowl. Then add the cream to the bowl and beat until almost stiff. Add the sugar and beat only until stiff peaks form. (If you overbeat, the cream will turn to butter.)

Sugar-Sifted Holiday Cookies and Brownies

(Photograph on page 94 and back of book jacket)

For food lovers, holidays are special. They are times when such people begin to think about baking, cooking, and eating. For them, here are several recipes for delicious, decoratively stenciled cookies and one for luscious brownies. To adorn the treats, there are six stencil designs from which to choose—each added with powdered cocoa or confectioner's sugar, depending on which contrasts best with the color of the background.

The idea of stenciling food is certainly not a new one. Mothers and grandmothers often sifted confectioner's sugar over a lace doily to embellish the top of a freshly baked cake. Later, paper doilies took the place of lace. A few years ago, I started using stencils professionally to decorate cookies, cakes, and other foods. Some of those designs are reproduced here for you, but if you feel they are too complicated to cut, you can still use a doily or a piece of lace, or you might even want simply to use decorative cookie cutters to create a visual effect. In any event, you will find the cookies and brownies delicious.

Walnut Tea Cookies

This delicious cookie dough holds its shape while baking and then absorbs its confectioner's-sugar topping to create its own frostinglike coating. Although the cocoa stenciling makes these cookies exceptionally beautiful, the designs are fragile, so handle them carefully.

MAKES 1 TO 1½ DOZEN, DEPENDING ON DESIGN

1 cup (2 sticks) unsalted butter, at room temperature
4 cups sifted confectioner's sugar
1 teaspoon vanilla extract
pinch of salt

2 cups all-purpose flour
½ cup finely chopped walnuts
about ¼ cup sifted cocoa for stenciling

1. In a large mixing bowl, cream the butter and 1 cup of the confectioner's sugar until light and fluffy. Beat in the vanilla, salt, and half the flour.

2. Stir in the remaining flour and the walnuts to make a stiff dough. Shape the dough into a flat round, wrap it tightly, and refrigerate overnight.

3. Remove the dough from the refrigerator and let it rest for 10 minutes before rolling it out. Preheat the oven to 350°F.

4. Lightly flour a rolling pin and your work surface. Turn the dough once on the floured surface to flour both sides and roll it out to a thickness slightly more than ⅛ inch. Using a paring knife and one of the cookie patterns, cut out as many cookies as possible. Gather the excess pieces of dough from around the cookies into a ball, wrap it tightly, and refrigerate until ready to make more cookies.

5. Using a lightly floured spatula, transfer the cookies to ungreased cookie sheets, leaving about 1 inch of space between cookies. Bake for about 12 minutes, or until the cookies are firm and the edges begin to brown slightly. Let them cool on the sheets for 2 minutes.

6. Meanwhile, place the remaining 3 cups of confectioner's sugar on a baking sheet with edges or in a 13- by 9-inch baking pan. Carefully place the cookies into the sugar, turning them several times so that both sides are evenly coated. Cool on wire racks to room temperature.

7. Remove the remaining dough from the refrigerator and repeat the process. When all the cookies have been baked, coated with sugar, and cooled to room temperature, sift the tops with the remaining confectioner's sugar, using a little more if necessary and working over a sheet of waxed paper to catch the excess sugar to be reused to coat the remaining cookies. Use the sifted cocoa to stencil the design on the cookies, following the stenciling instructions.

Chocolate Cream-Cheese Cookies

The combining of chocolate with cream cheese gives these cookies an extraordinary flavor. After the cookies have been cut and baked, they are stenciled with confectioner's sugar and one of the whimsical designs.

MAKES 1 TO 1½ DOZEN, DEPENDING ON DESIGN

1 cup (2 sticks) unsalted butter, at room temperature
1 package (8 ounces) cream cheese, at room temperature
1 cup sugar
pinch of salt
3 tablespoons cocoa
3½ cups all-purpose flour
sifted confectioner's sugar for stenciling

1. In a large mixing bowl, beat the butter and cream cheese together until fluffy; add the sugar, salt, and cocoa and beat the mixture until well blended. Stir in half the flour and mix until smooth. Blend in the remaining flour to make a stiff dough. Shape the dough into a flat round, wrap it tightly, and refrigerate overnight.

2. Remove the dough from the refrigerator and let it rest for 10 minutes before rolling it out. Preheat the oven to 350°F.

3. Lightly flour a rolling pin and your work surface. Turn the dough once on the floured surface to flour both sides and roll it out to a thickness slightly more than ⅛ inch. Using a paring knife and one of the cookie patterns, cut out as many cookies as possible. Gather the excess pieces of dough from around the cookies into a ball, wrap it tightly, and refrigerate until ready to make more cookies.

4. Using a lightly floured spatula, transfer the cookies to ungreased cookie sheets, leaving about 1 inch of space between cookies. Bake until the cookies are firm and the edges begin to brown, about 15 minutes. Cool the cookies on the sheets for about 5 minutes and then transfer them to wire racks to cool. Remove the remaining dough from the refrigerator and repeat the rolling and cutting-out process. Make sure that the baking sheets are cool before placing the unbaked cookies on them. Use the sifted confectioner's sugar to stencil the design on the cookies, following the stenciling instructions.

Gingerbread Cookies

There are two kinds of gingerbread—the kind that is soft and cakelike and this type, which is sturdy and crisp like a cookie. Designs stenciled with confectioner's sugar show up well over the deep color of the cookies.

MAKES 1 TO 1½ DOZEN, DEPENDING ON DESIGN

10 tablespoons (1 stick plus 2 tablespoons) unsalted butter, at room temperature
¾ cup sugar
1 egg
⅓ cup molasses
3 cups all-purpose flour
½ teaspoon baking soda
¼ teaspoon salt
2 teaspoons cinnamon
1 teaspoon powdered ginger
sifted confectioner's sugar for stenciling

1. In a large mixing bowl, cream together the butter and sugar. Add the egg and molasses, beating the mixture until light and fluffy. Stir in half the flour and all the baking soda, salt, cinnamon, and ginger. Blend in the remaining flour to make a stiff dough. Shape the dough into a flat round, wrap it tightly, and refrigerate overnight.

2. Remove the dough from the refrigerator and let it rest for 10 minutes before rolling it out. Preheat the oven to 325°F.

3. Lightly flour a rolling pin and your work surface. Turn the dough once on the floured surface to flour both sides. Roll the dough out to a thickness slightly more than ⅛ inch. Using a paring knife and one of the cookie patterns, cut out as many cookies as possible. Gather the excess pieces of dough from around the cookies into a ball, wrap it tightly, and refrigerate it until needed.

4. Using a lightly floured spatula, transfer the cookies to ungreased cookie sheets, leaving about 1 inch of space between cookies. Bake until the cookies are firm and the edges begin to brown, about 15 minutes. Cool the cookies on the sheets for 5 minutes and then transfer them to wire racks to cool. Remove the remaining dough from the refrigerator and repeat the process. Make sure that the baking sheets are cool before placing the unbaked cookies on them. Use the sifted confectioner's sugar to stencil the design on the cookies, following the stenciling instructions.

Fresh Orange Butter Cookies

Grated orange rind adds a fine flavor to this simple butter-cookie recipe, or, if you prefer, substitute lemon rind for the orange rind—the results will be equally delicious.
MAKES 1 TO 1½ DOZEN, DEPENDING ON DESIGN

10 *tablespoons (1 stick plus 2 tablespoons) unsalted butter, at room temperature*	3 *cups all-purpose flour*
¾ *cup sugar*	½ *teaspoon baking soda*
1 *egg*	¼ *teaspoon salt*
⅓ *cup light corn syrup*	1 *tablespoon grated fresh orange rind*
	sifted cocoa for stenciling

1. In a large mixing bowl, cream together the butter and sugar. Add the egg and corn syrup, beating the mixture until light and fluffy.

2. Stir in half the flour and all the baking soda, salt, and orange rind. Stir in the remaining flour to make a stiff dough. Shape the dough into a flat round, wrap it tightly, and refrigerate overnight.

3. Remove the dough from the refrigerator and let it rest for 10 minutes before rolling it out. Preheat the oven to 325°F.

4. Lightly flour a rolling pin and your work surface. Turn the dough once on the floured surface to flour both sides and roll it out to a thickness slightly more than ⅛ inch. Using a paring knife and one of the cookie patterns, cut out as many cookies as possible. Gather the excess pieces of dough from around the cookies into a ball, wrap it tightly, and refrigerate until needed.

5. Using a lightly floured spatula, transfer the cookies to ungreased cookie sheets, leaving about 1 inch of space between cookies. Bake until the cookies are firm and the edges begin to brown, about 15 minutes. Cool the cookies on the sheets for 5 minutes and then transfer them to wire racks to cool. Remove the remaining dough from the refrigerator and repeat the process. Make sure that the baking sheets are cool before placing the unbaked cookies on them. Use the

sifted cocoa to stencil the design on the cookies, following the stenciling instructions.

Peppermint Butter Cookies

A few drops of peppermint extract give these light and crispy cookies a flavor that, perhaps, will remind you of your childhood. They are pretty when tinted pale pink, but equally good when left their natural color.

MAKES 1 TO 1½ DOZEN, DEPENDING ON DESIGN

1 cup (2 sticks) unsalted butter, at room temperature
1 cup sifted confectioner's sugar
¼ teaspoon baking soda
¼ teaspoon cream of tartar
4 drops peppermint extract

2 to 3 drops red food coloring (optional)
2¼ cups all-purpose flour
about ¼ cup sifted cocoa for stenciling

1. In a large mixing bowl, cream the butter and confectioner's sugar until light and fluffy. Beat in the baking soda, cream of tartar, peppermint extract, and the optional food coloring. Stir in about half of the flour until well blended. Stir in the remaining flour to make a stiff dough. Shape the dough into a flat round, wrap it tightly, and refrigerate overnight.

2. Remove the dough from the refrigerator and let it rest for 10 minutes before rolling it out. Preheat the oven to 350°F.

3. Lightly flour a rolling pin and your work surface. Turn the dough once on the floured surface to flour both sides and roll it out to a thickness slightly more than ⅛ inch. Using a paring knife and one of the cookie patterns, cut out as many cookies as possible. Gather the excess pieces of dough from around the cookies into a ball, wrap it tightly, and refrigerate until needed.

4. Using a lightly floured spatula, transfer the cookies to ungreased cookie sheets, leaving about 1 inch of space between cookies. Bake until the cookies are firm and the edges begin to brown, about 12 minutes. Cool the cookies on the sheets for about 5 minutes and then transfer them to wire racks to cool. Remove the remaining dough from the refrigerator and repeat the process. Make sure that the baking sheets are cool before placing the unbaked cookies on them. Use the sifted cocoa to stencil the design, following the stenciling instructions.

Chocolate-Walnut Brownies

These rich and moist brownies can be made with or without the addition of walnuts. After they have been cut into squares or rectangles, following the patterns, they are stenciled with confectioner's sugar.

MAKES 4 OR 8 BROWNIES, DEPENDING ON DESIGN

2 tablespoons unsalted butter, at room temperature
1 cup (2 sticks) unsalted butter, sliced
5 squares (1 ounce each) unsweetened chocolate

4 eggs
¼ teaspoon salt
2 cups sugar
1 tablespoon vanilla extract
1 cup all-purpose flour
1½ cups chopped walnuts

1. Preheat the oven to 325°F. Using part of the softened butter, lightly coat a 13- by 9-inch baking pan and line it, crosswise, with waxed paper. Using the remaining softened butter, coat the paper and pan ends; set aside.

2. Place the 1 cup sliced butter and the chocolate in the top portion of a double-boiler set over simmering water. Stir occasionally until the butter and chocolate have melted; remove from the heat. Scrape the chocolate mixture into a small, heatproof bowl to cool slightly.

3. In a large mixing bowl, beat the eggs and salt together until just blended. Gradually add the sugar as you continue to beat. When the mixture is fluffy and light in color, stir in the chocolate mixture and the vanilla. Beat in the flour until the mixture is just smooth and then stir in the walnuts. Pour into the prepared pan and bake in the center of the oven for about 40 minutes; a toothpick inserted in the center will come out almost clean. (Do not overbake or the brownies will be dry.) Let cool in the pan and then refrigerate until chilled.

4. Using a knife, loosen the edge of the brownie all around. Place a rack over the pan and then invert both together so that the brownie inverts onto the rack. Remove the pan, peel off the waxed paper, and trim ⅛ to ¼ inch from the edge all around. Using either the square pattern or the rectangular pattern for size, cut the brownie into squares or rectangles. Using sifted confectioner's sugar, stencil the brownies according to the following procedure.

How to Make Stencils and Patterns

Materials needed:
fine-tipped black marking pen
tracing paper
glue, preferably spray glue
posterboard
scissors
waxed stencil paper
masking tape
X-acto knife with #11 blade
lightweight cardboard

1. To make stencils: Using the marking pen, trace the desired stencil pattern onto the tracing paper. The areas that are solid black are the areas to be cut away to make the stencil (the dotted line around each is the pattern for the cookie—see step 5).

2. Glue the tracing paper, coating it well all over, to the sheet of posterboard and let the glue dry.

3. With scissors, cut a piece of stencil paper 1 inch larger all around than the design and tape it over the design.

4. To cut the stencil, use the X-acto knife, holding it as you would a pencil, and cut toward yourself, rotating the posterboard as necessary and cutting out along the outer edge of each solid black shape. Always making sure that the X-acto blade is sharp, cut out the shapes, working in the center first and cutting through the stencil paper with one clean stroke. When all the shapes have been cut out, remove the tape and stencil. If you have severed any of the areas of stencil paper between the cutout shapes, apply a small piece of transparent tape to both front and back so that the stencil will hold together; cut away any excess tape.

5. To make patterns: Using tracing paper and a pencil or pen, trace the dotted line around each stencil pattern. Cut the tracing-paper shape out with scissors and draw around the outline on the cardboard; cut out the shape with scissors.

How to Stencil Cookies and Brownies

Materials needed:
large plate or platter
wire sieve
sifted cocoa or confectioner's sugar
fine-pointed paintbrush

1. Place one cooled, baked cookie on a plate and center the corresponding stencil over it (the border you left will prevent the cocoa or sugar from sifting onto the cookie's edge).

2. Holding the sieve in one hand 3 to 4 inches above the stencil, begin moving it back and forth over the stencil as you sprinkle cocoa or confectioner's sugar into it. Do not add too much cocoa or sugar or you will have difficulty picking the stencil up.

3. With steady hands, carefully lift the stencil straight up. (If you have stenciled with confectioner's sugar and your design didn't come out as neatly as you'd like, you can dip the tip of the paintbrush into water and "paint' away the mistakes.) Carefully set the cookie aside so that the butter content of the cookies will have time to "adhere" the design. Continue stenciling the remaining cookies in the same manner.

COOKIE AND BROWNIE PATTERNS

Cornucopia with Cream Puffs and Chocolate Sauce

(Photograph on page 91)

Although this crispy cornucopia, overflowing with light and airy cream puffs, is quite time-consuming to make, especially if you make the puff pastry from scratch, it makes such an elegant and dramatic centerpiece for any dessert table that the effort is worth it. The cornucopia is made of strips of puff pastry *(pâte feuilletée)* wrapped around an aluminum-foil cone, and the cream puffs inside are made of puff paste *(pâte à choux)*, a moist egg dough that puffs like magic in the oven. The puffs are then filled with a pastry cream drenched with orange-flavored liqueur and vanilla, which complements the flavor of the chocolate sauce that is served over them. (If desired, the cream puffs can also be filled with slightly sweetened whipped cream or any number of other sweet fillings.)

For display purposes, you might arrange the cream puffs in the cornucopia before they are filled and then fill them no more than an hour before serving time. To serve, place two or three of the puffs on each guest's plate and accompany them with the Chocolate Sauce. The crispy, sugar-coated cornucopia itself, with its many layers of flaky, buttery pastry, is also delicious—simply break off the pieces.

French Puff Pastry (*Pâte Feuilletée*)

Choose a cool, dry day on which to prepare this pastry and allow the full day because there are a number of resting and chilling stages necessary. Traditionally, puff pastry is made on a marble surface because marble is cooler than other work surfaces, but rolling a bag of ice around on a formica or butcher-block surface will also work to cool it enough. It is then necessary to make sure that the surface is completely dry before rolling the pastry.

MAKES ABOUT 1½ POUNDS

¾ teaspoon salt
½ cup cold water
1 cup all-purpose flour
¾ cup plain cake flour or all-purpose flour

3 tablespoons unsalted butter, at room temperature
1 cup (2 sticks) unsalted butter, chilled

1. In a small bowl, dissolve the salt in the water and refrigerate. In a medium-size bowl, combine the all-purpose flour and the cake flour. Using two knives or a pastry blender, cut in the softened butter until the mixture resembles coarse meal. Quickly rub the mixture between your fingertips to blend, about 30 seconds. Stir in the reserved salt water with a fork only until the dough can be gathered into a ball. Working quickly, knead the dough for about 5 seconds and then flatten it into a 5-inch round. Place it in a plastic bag or wrap it tightly in plastic wrap and refrigerate for 2 hours.

2. Lay over your work surface a sheet of heavy-duty aluminum foil that measures 18 by 36 inches. Fold it in half to make an 18-inch square. Place the two sticks of chilled butter next to each other, directly in the center of the foil. Fold all four sides up over the butter to make a rectangle 5 by 7 inches. Working quickly so that the butter softens but remains very cold, beat the package all over with a rolling pin until the butter also forms a 5- by 7-inch rectangle; refrigerate until needed.

3. Unwrap the chilled dough, lightly flour it and your work surface, and roll the dough out, preferably with a large, heavy rolling pin, to a 12-inch round. Unwrap the chilled butter rectangle and place it in the center of the dough. Fold the dough upward all around the butter, pinching it together to completely encase the butter. Quickly roll the dough out to a rectangle that measures 8 by 14 inches (see illus. A-1). (If the dough should soften too much during any of the following rolling processes, return it to the refrigerator until chilled. Also, if any butter protrudes through the dough as you roll, pinch the dough together in that spot with a bit of flour.) Starting with one short end, fold one-third of the dough inward (see illus. A-2) and then fold the other end over the one you just folded (see illus. A-3). Again lightly flour the dough and your work surface and, working very quickly, again roll the dough into a rectangle 8 by 14 inches; fold it into thirds as you did previously. Place the dough in a plastic bag or wrap it well in aluminum foil and chill for 1 hour, or until the dough is cold, firm, and the gluten content of the flour has relaxed.

4. Remove the dough from the refrigerator, unwrap it, and lightly flour both sides. On a lightly floured surface, roll it again to an 8- by 14-inch rectangle; fold into thirds. Working quickly, repeat the rolling and folding process in the same way. Wrap the dough well and chill it for 1½ hours.

5. Repeat step 4 once more so that you have rolled and folded the dough a total of six times. Wrap the dough well and refrigerate it for 2 hours or more, or until firm and cold. Although the dough will puff to its maximum at this stage, it can be held in the refrigerator for as long as two or three days.

ILLUSTRATION A-1 **ILLUSTRATION A-2** **ILLUSTRATION A-3**

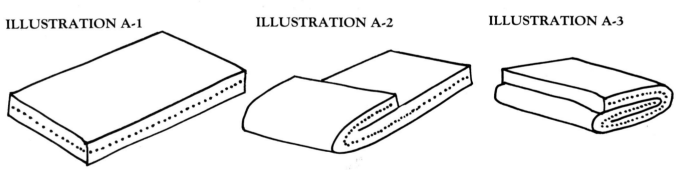

Puff Pastry Cornucopia
This cornucopia can be prepared a day or two ahead of time and then stored in a dry place, such as a cold oven or a large, airtight container.

MAKES ONE 10- TO 12-INCH CORNUCOPIA

1 *tablespoon unsalted butter, at*	1 *egg, lightly beaten*
room temperature	1 *tablespoon sugar*
2 *teaspoons vegetable oil*	
1¼ *to 1½ pounds French Puff Pastry*	
(recipe precedes)	

1. Cut four 18-inch squares of heavy-duty aluminum foil and one rectangle that measures 18 by 36 inches. Crumple the rectangle into a ball and set it aside while

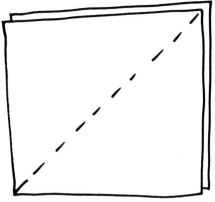

you shape the cone. Place one 18-inch square on top of a second sheet (see illus. B-1) and fold them together to make a triangle (see illus. B-2); repeat with the remaining two 18-inch squares. Roll one of the triangles into a cone shape (see illus. B-3), overlapping the seam (see illus. B-4). Repeat with the remaining triangle and insert one cone into the other with the seams opposite each other and crimp the edge inward all around to strengthen the form. Then coat the outside of the cone with the softened butter. Also rub a baking sheet with the oil and set it aside.

ILLUSTRATION B-2   ILLUSTRATION B-3

ILLUSTRATION B-4

2. Remove the puff pastry from the refrigerator, cut off one-third of it, and return the remainder, wrapped, to the refrigerator. Lightly flour your work surface, the dough, and a heavy rolling pin. Roll the pastry out, turning it over occasionally, to make a rectangle about 8 by 15 inches that is slightly more than ⅛ inch thick. Using a long, sharp knife and cutting downward (do not saw), trim the dough to measure 7½ by 14 inches (if desired, reserve the scraps, without combining them, wrap them, and refrigerate—they can be cut into shapes and baked later to make little hors d'oeuvre). Then cut the dough into five strips, each measuring 1½ by 14 inches.

3. Beginning at the point of the foil cone and working toward the opening, wrap one strip at a time around it. As you wrap, brush ¼ inch of the lower edge of the strip above with some of the beaten egg and gently press into position (see illus. C-1). When you need to add another strip, brush some of the egg on the end you are beginning with, lap it ¼ inch over the end of the last strip, gently press in place, and continue winding (see illus. C-2). As you work, place one hand inside the cone to help support the cone. When all five strips have been used, roll out one-third more of the refrigerated dough (return the remainder to the refrigerator), cut into five 1½- by 14-inch strips, and continue wrapping the cone. When you have wrapped one-third to half of the cone, insert the crumpled foil ball into the cone to help support the weight of the dough. When the second five strips have been used, adjust an oven rack so that it is in the lower third of the oven and preheat the oven to 425°F. Then complete wrapping the cornucopia with the remaining third of the dough in the same way.

4. Place the cornucopia on one side on the prepared baking sheet (see illus. C-3), flattening that side slightly to become the bottom. Brush the top with more of the egg and then sprinkle it evenly with the sugar. Bake in the lower third of the oven for 10 to 15 minutes, or until the cornucopia has puffed and begun to turn a light golden brown. Reduce the heat to 375°F. and continue baking another 10 to 15 minutes, or until it is crisp and golden brown (if the top is browning too quickly, cover it loosely with a piece of crumpled aluminum foil). Remove the cornucopia from the oven and reduce the temperature to 300°F. Let the cornucopia rest for 5 minutes and then remove and discard the crumpled ball of foil, using potholders. Next, carefully remove the foil cone, twisting it gently if necessary; discard the foil. Return the cone still on the baking sheet to the oven and bake it slowly for about 20 minutes to dry out the puff pastry. Transfer to a wire rack and let it cool.

ILLUSTRATION C-1

ILLUSTRATION C-2

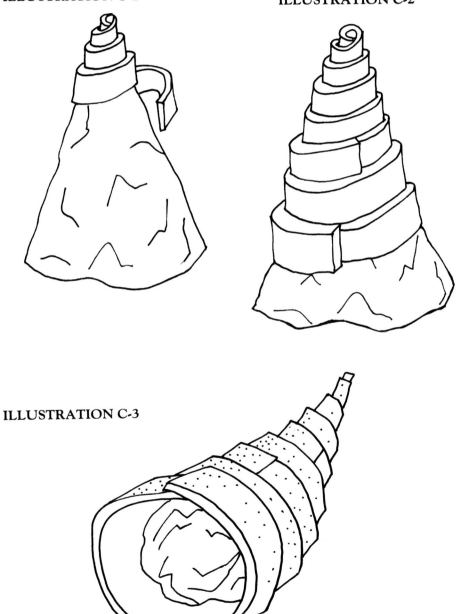

ILLUSTRATION C-3

Cream Puffs (Pâte à Choux)

These small cream puffs can be made a day or two before serving and stored in a dry place, such as a cold oven or an airtight container. The unfilled puffs are then arranged to spill out of the Puff Pastry Cornucopia as the centerpiece for your dinner table or dessert table. Up to one hour before serving, the puffs are filled with Pastry Cream or slightly sweetened whipped cream and chilled. Add a dab of Chocolate Sauce, which should be made no longer than six hours ahead, and serve.

MAKES ABOUT 30 TWO-INCH CREAM PUFFS

½ cup (1 stick) unsalted butter,
    sliced
¼ teaspoon salt
1 teaspoon sugar
1 cup all-purpose flour

4 large eggs, at room temperature
3 cups Pastry Cream (recipe
    follows) or sweetened whipped
    cream

1. Prepare the cream puffs: Preheat the oven to 450°F. Lightly grease and flour two baking sheets, tapping off the excess flour.

2. Place 1 cup water in a heavy, medium-size saucepan along with the butter, salt, and sugar. Bring the mixture to a boil over moderately high heat, stirring occasionally to melt the butter. Remove from the heat and add the flour all at once; quickly beat with a wooden spoon until well blended. Place the pan over low heat and beat until the mixture forms a smooth, cohesive ball, about 2 minutes. Remove from the heat. One at a time, beat the eggs in, making sure that each is well blended before adding another. When the paste is complete, it should be smooth and soft enough to cling to the sides of the pan. If you do not want to use the paste immediately, cover it with plastic and keep at room temperature for as long as 4 to 5 hours or refrigerate it for as long as 48 hours and then allow it to come to room temperature before using.

3. Although the paste can be dropped by spoonfuls onto the prepared baking sheets, they will look more professional if you pipe them from a pastry bag. Fit a pastry bag with a plain ½-inch tip and fill it no more than halfway with the paste. Working on the prepared baking sheets, squeeze out balls of paste about the size of walnuts, leaving 1 inch of space between them. To squeeze out the paste, start by placing the tip of the pastry bag very close to the baking sheet; as you squeeze, slowly raise the tip no more than ½ to ¾ inch from the sheet and hold it there until the desired size has been reached. To finish, rotate the tip to produce a rounded top with a flat swirl on it. Continue filling the bag halfway with the paste and squeezing out balls until the baking sheets are full and no paste remains.

4. Bake the balls 8 to 10 minutes, or until puffed and slightly golden. Reduce the heat to 400°F. and bake another 5 minutes. Reduce the heat to 300°F. and bake 10 minutes, or until golden brown and hard. Remove the sheets of puffs from the oven and reduce the oven temperature to 250°F. Using a chopstick or a knife point, make a hole about ¼ inch in diameter at the side of each if you will be filling the puffs with Pastry Cream or closer to the top if you will be piping whipped cream into them. Return the puffs to the oven for about 10 minutes to dry their interiors. Remove and cool to room temperature.

5. Fill the cream puffs: Fit a pastry bag with a plain or star tip with a ¼-inch diameter. Half-fill the bag with the Pastry Cream or sweetened whipped cream. Insert the tip into the hole of one puff and squeeze until the interior is full.

Repeat with the remaining puffs and Pastry Cream or whipped cream. Serve within an hour so that the filling is still cold. To serve, place two or three cream puffs on each guest's plate and spoon about 1½ teaspoons of the Chocolate Sauce over each or serve the sauce on the side in a bowl or sauce boat.

Pastry Cream

This Pastry Cream has been flavored with orange liqueur and vanilla, but you might want to experiment with other flavor combinations. The Pastry Cream can be made as long as two days in advance and refrigerated, but it must be chilled at least overnight and it should be piped into the cream puffs no earlier than an hour before serving time. If the day is a hot one, wait until the last minute.

MAKES 3 CUPS (enough to fill about 30 Cream Puffs)

7 egg yolks	2 teaspoons vanilla extract
⅔ cup sugar	3 tablespoons orange-flavored
⅔ cup all-purpose flour	liqueur, such as Grand Marnier,
2½ cups milk	Cointreau, or Triple Sec

1. Place the egg yolks and sugar in a medium-size, heatproof bowl and whisk or beat the mixture for 1 to 2 minutes, or until it is light in color. Stir in the flour until well blended, cover, and set aside.

2. Place the milk in a heavy, medium-size saucepan set over moderate heat and, stirring frequently, bring the milk just to a boil; the surface will be foamy and rise about 1 inch. Take care not to scorch the milk (if this begins to happen, reduce the heat immediately or transfer to another saucepan and continue).

3. Using a whisk or an electric mixer, slowly beat the hot milk into the egg-yolk mixture. Transfer the hot mixture to another heavy, medium-size pan and place it over moderate heat. Stirring constantly, bring the mixture to a boil; the pastry cream should have thickened. Beating constantly, boil the pastry cream for 3 minutes to cook the flour. (Because of the flour content, there is no need to worry about the egg yolks curdling.) Remove from the heat and stir in the vanilla and orange-flavored liqueur. Cover with a sheet of plastic wrap or waxed paper placed directly on the surface to prevent the pastry cream from forming a film on the surface. Cool to room temperature and refrigerate, covered, at least overnight.

Chocolate Sauce for Cream Puffs

Although this sauce was developed to spoon over the cream puffs, it is equally good when served warm over homemade vanilla ice cream. Prepare the sauce the day you are to serve it—if left overnight, it will solidify.

MAKES ABOUT 1 CUP (enough for 30 Cream Puffs)

½ cup milk	7 squares (1 ounce each) semisweet
3 tablespoons sugar	chocolate, cut into small pieces

Place the milk, sugar, and chocolate in a small, heavy saucepan over low heat. Stirring frequently, heat until the chocolate has melted and the sauce is very smooth. Remove from the heat. Cool to room temperature. If the sauce should solidify before you are ready to serve it, reheat it in the top of a double-boiler and then cool to room temperature.

Index